PHOTOGRAPHING FUNGI IN THE FIELD

George McCarthy

Amanita muscaria

PHOTOGRAPHING FUNGI IN THE FIELD

George McCarthy

First published 2001 by
Guild of Master Craftsman Publications Ltd,
166 High Street, Lewes,
East Sussex, BN7 1XN

Text and photographs © George McCarthy 2001
Copyright in the Work © Guild of Master Craftsman Publications Ltd

ISBN 1 86108 236 3

A catalogue record of this book is available from the British Library.

Original design and edit by Grant Bradford
Original text by Sara Shipley
Cover design by Ian Smith and Samantha Reeves and additional design by Olly Prentice,
GMC Publications Ltd Studio

Typeface: Cochin

Colour origination by MRM Graphics

Printed and bound by Kyodo Printing (Singapore)
under the supervision of MRM Graphics, Winslow, Buckinghamshire, UK

Dedicated to Ella and Sam

Contents

Introduction

Macrolepiota procera
Parasol Mushroom

A large imposing mushroom with a cap that can grow to the size of a dinner plate. The cap is more or less flattened when mature, brownish-white covered with dark scales and showing a solid brown central patch. The stem has zig-zag snake like markings on it, a moveable ring and a bulbous base. The gills are creamy-white and crowded. It grows in grassland and by roads and paths from late summer onwards.

*Cap 10-25cm. Stem 15-25cm.
Common.*
Edible and good.

This book is designed as a celebration of the beauty, ingenuity, mystery and power of fungi. No spore measurements here; just an invitation to discover more about these incredible and magical plants, their history and the folklore which surrounds them.

Recently there has been a great upsurge of interest in the study of mushrooms and toadstools. Consequently there has been an amazing proliferation of Field Guides devoted to helping the interested amateur mycologist (one who studies fungi) identify some of the thousands of species which can be found in this country. These range from the minute rusts, smuts and moulds which grow on leaves, stale bread, fruit, etc. to mushrooms like the aptly named 'Parasol' which can grow to the size of a dinner plate, and the large woody brackets found on old and dead trees. Over 3,000 of these larger fungi are what are commonly known as mushrooms and toadstools.

Trying to identify something be it plant, bird or animal is a fascinating pastime and carries with it all the thrills of a detective story. But how often do we cease to see and appreciate what had previously fascinated us once a satisfactory conclusion has been reached. Once an object is labelled we tend to pigeonhole and file it away and it is no longer a source of wonder to us.

Fungi have been around for a very long time. Some say 370 million years as evidenced by the finds in Rhynie bog made earlier this century. Others argue that the first recognisable fossil was found in pre-Cambrian rock some 1,000 million years ago. Fungi being soft bodied do not make ideal fossil material and not many are found, which makes the few that do see the light of day all the more remarkable.

History

References to fungi appear in many writings throughout history and are not always complimentary. In 185 BC, the physician Nicander described them as being 'the evil ferment of the earth' and he warned against picking any that grew

Boletus erythropus

near the roots of oak or olive but those near fig trees were deemed to be safe. (Reading this centuries later, the Roman, Pliny, wondered how one could tell which is which when they are on the market stall)!

Indeed Pliny had plenty to say on the subject including 'The origin of boletus is from mud and the acrid juices of moist earth, or frequently from those of acorn bearing trees'. He also described two kinds of fungi - one that was 'Sandy and injured the teeth'. The second was 'without any foreign matter'.

The Roman Poet, Horace, suggested 'The meadow mushrooms are in kind the best; it is ill trusting any of the rest,' and Dioscorides, whose De Materia Medica was to become a point of reference and discussion for herbalists hundreds of years later, warned that fungi 'if partaken of too freely are injurious being indigestible…'

Although the Greeks and Romans appear to have known and appreciated both the edible and poisonous properties of various types of fungi, how they came to germinate and grow was a mystery to them. One seriously considered theory was that they were brought into being as the result of

Boletus erythropus
Red-Stalked Boletus

Quite common and widespread in deciduous and coniferous woodland. Initially the pores are yellow but with age become a vivid red. This mushroom although edible when cooked should not be consumed with alcohol. Cap 5-20cm. Stem 5-15cm. Common.
Can cause stomach upsets.

Abortiporus biennis

This is an unusual and very variable shaped bracket fungus. The flesh, which is at first white, grows fused together forming rosette shaped caps and eventually turns pink. It grows during the summer through to autumn. Fruit body 3-9cm across.
Uncommon. **Inedible.**

Abortiporus biennis

Xerocomus parasiticus

Lycoperdon echinatum
Hedgehog Puffball

The fruit body is white at first becoming brown as it matures. It is covered with spines which are eventually shed and in common with other puffballs. It grows in deciduous woodland and on heaths. Fruit body 2-6cm. Uncommon.
Inedible.

Xerocomus parasiticus
Parasitic Bolete

This tiny boletus species grows exclusively on the common earthball Scleroderma citrinum. The pores are lemon yellow but darken to rusty brown with age. It is a rare fungus in Britain found from late summer onwards.
Cap 2-4cm. Stem 1-4cm. Rare.
Should not be picked.

Lycoperdon echinatum

thunderstorms. This idea apparently applied to truffles. Fungi remained a mystery for many centuries and during that time filled a dual role being both feared and shunned and yet at the same time providing prized delicacies for the table.

The Herbalists of the 16th Century, though mainly still basing their ideas on those of Dioscorides 1500 years earlier, were beginning to come up with new thoughts and observations. An interesting statement comes from Caesalpinus who notes 'Some plants have no seed; these are the most imperfect and spring from decaying substances ... they are a sort of intermediate existence between plants and inanimate nature. In this respect fungi resemble zoophytes which are intermediate between plants and animals.' This idea was well ahead of its time and is one which is exercising the minds of mycologists and scientists today.

Charles de L'Ecluse gives illustrated descriptions in his *Historia rariorum plantarum* of over 40 different fungi - he divides them into edible and poisonous species, but many which he considered to be poisonous, such as some of the Boletes, we know today to be edible. However, this was the first time that fungi had been described so specifically.

Scleroderma citrinum

Scleroderma citrinum
Common Earthball

The fruit body of this widespread and common fungus is stemless, round and leathery and covered with coarse scales. In maturing the flesh becomes thin finally splitting to allow the spores to escape. It is found growing on the soil in woodlands, commons and heathlands from late summer onwards.
Fruit body 3-12cm. Common.
Inedible.

Langermannia gigantea
Giant Puffball

There is no mistaking this fungus for any other simply by its size. Full grown specimens can exceed a staggering 20kg in weight and possess a diameter of 100cm. It is a widespread and occasional fungus in Britain growing from late summer in meadows, pastures, woodlands and, as here, in stinging nettles. There was a memorable time when motorists travelling to and from London Airport would have seen literally hundreds growing in the central reservation of the M25. I am quite sure that many of the drivers that saw them must have wondered what on earth they were!
It is a good edible species when young provided the flesh is white throughout.

Langermannia gigantea

Lycoperdon perlatum
Common Puffball

This is one situation where I had to take the fungi into the studio in order to show the spore dispersal common to puffballs, earthballs and earth stars. As the fruit body matures and the spores are ready the flesh becomes paper thin, eventually rupturing in a central opening or pore. The spores are released in brown clouds, a you see here, by the splashing action of raindrops or when disturbed by animals including man.
Fruit body 2-6cm. Common.
Edible when young.

Otidea onotica

Otidea onotica
Hare's Ear

I was delighted when I found this group of fruit bodies growing by the side of a path bordering mixed woodland. Each individual fruit body is cup or 'ear' shaped with an inrolled margin and both inner and outer surfaces are yellow, usually with a pink flush. Fruit body 3-6cm. Uncommon.
Inedible.

Otidea bufonia
Pig's Ear

The fruit body is cup shaped with a wavy margin and split on one side. The outer surface is pale brown, the inner much darker. It can be found in the grass of woodlands, roadside verges and as here, in garden lawns. Fruit body 1-7cm. Uncommon.
Inedible.

Otidea bufonia

Aleuria aurantia

Aleuria aurantia
Orange Peel Fungus

A widespread and fairly common fungus from June onwards. Usually several fruit bodies can be found growing on bare or sandy ground. The flesh is wax-like and delicate, forming wavy or irregular cup shapes. The orange to red flesh makes this fungus easy to recognise. Cup 4-15cm. Stemless. Common. **Edible.**

Clavariadelphus pistillaris
Giant Club

This is a rare fungus in Britain where it appears during the autumn on chalky soil under beech. I visited this site three years running before I found this lone specimen camouflaged in the leaf litter. Fruit body 7-30cm. Rare. **Inedible.**

Peziza petersii

The fruit body is cup shaped with rusty-buff inner and outer surfaces, greyer towards the base. It is often found growing closely grouped together on burnt wood or bonfire sites. Fruit body 2-5cm. Uncommon. **Inedible.**

Peziza petersii

Cortinarius trivialis

Cortinarius amoenolens

Cortinarius auroturbinatus

Cortinarius trivialis

Probably the most obvious feature distinguishing this toadstool is that it always appears viscid (slimy and sticky). The stem often has several rings of slime which merge together in wet weather. It is fairly common appearing in autumn growing in the wetter areas of deciduous woodlands. Cap 3-8cm. Stem 5-10cm. Occasional. **Inedible.**

Cortinarius amoenolens
Fruity Cortinarius

The cap is straw coloured with gills that are initially blue changing to chocolate brown with age. The stout stem is white with tinges of blue at the top and the characteristic rounded bulb at the base. It is common in Britain under broadleaved trees, especially beech, during the autumn. Cap 5-15cm. Stem 5-10cm. Common. **Not edible.**

Cortinarius auroturbinatus

The cap surface is bright chrome yellow which sometimes shows a reddish centre. The gills too are lemon yellow becoming brownish with age. This is quite a rare fungus in Britain confined to southern beechwoods and found from late summer through into autumn. Cap 5-12cm. Stem 5-12cm. Rare. **Inedible.**

Cortinarius sanguineus
Blood-Red Cortinarius

This gorgeous little toadstool is uniformly blood-red in the cap, gills and stem. The cap is covered with silky fibrils and is at first convex becoming flattened with age. It is found mainly in coniferous woodlands during the autumn. Cap 2-6cm. Stem 2-6cm. Rare. **Not edible.**

Cortinarius sanguineus

In the 17th century, Gerard had much to say about mushrooms, not a great deal of it flattering, as in '…some are venomous, others not so noisome, and neither of them very wholesome meat.' Or the gloomy 'few mushrooms are good to be eaten and most of them do suffocate and strangle the eater…' Although he wasn't the first to do so, Gerard included pictures in his famous Herbal of 1638 explaining that 'Whereof for the avoiding of the venomous qualities of the one and that the other which is less venomous may be discovered, I have thought to set forth their pictures with their names and places of growth'.

He does, however, allow Jews Ear (Auricularia auricula-judea) a good press and recommends a concoction of this

Agaricus campestris

Agaricus campestris
Field Mushroom

Not as common as it once was it grows in grassland preferably meadows and pastures grazed by horses. The mushroom is white with pink to dark brown gills which are the main feature separating it from the Death Cap. It is often found in groups or forms rings from early summer and is an excellent edible species although you might prefer not to eat those shown in these pictures! Cap 2-10cm. Stem 3-8cm. Common.
Edible and excellent.

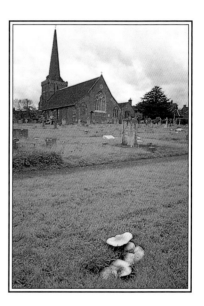

which has been 'boiled in milke, steeped in beere, vinegar or any other convenient liquor.' for sore throats and other 'inflammations'. Gerard also talks about the practice of burning 'Fusse Balls' or Puff balls. 'County people do use to kill or smother Bees with these Fusse-balls being set a fire, for which purpose they fitly severth'. This practice is one which modern bee keepers know about as smoke is known to make a swarm drowsy and more controllable.

The advent of the microscope led to more detailed observations, in 1665 Robert Hooke published his 'Micographia' in which he discusses, amongst many other things, a rose blight and several moulds. But despite 'modern technology' Hooke still held to the view that '…mould and mushrooms require no seminal property but the former may be produced at any time from any kind of putrefying Animal and Vegetable substance, as Flesh, etc and kept warm…'. Surprisingly he did not notice spores on any of the moulds he looked at or, more probably, he did not recognise them for what they were.

Agaricus augustus
The Prince

The pale brown cap of this attractive mushroom is covered with small fibrous golden scales. The gills are initially pink, changing to brown, and supported by a comparatively slim white stem which displays a very obvious ring. It grows in deciduous and conifer woodland, parks and on roadside verges which is where I photographed these fine specimens. It smells of bitter almonds but do not let that put you off - it tastes delicious and is aptly named. Cap 10-18cm. Stem 12-20cm. Summer to Autumn. Uncommon. **Edible and excellent**

Agaricus haemorrhoidarius

Agaricus augustus

Agaricus haemorrhoidarius

A rare wood mushroom growing in the soil of broad-leaved woodlands usually in large trooping groups. When cut the flesh turns bright red and the smell is non-specific. The gills are initially pink turning dark brown to black with maturity. The unfortunate choice of Latin name detracts somewhat from its excellent taste!

Edible and excellent.

Note: Great care should be taken with any Agaricus that bruises or stains yellow.

Folklore

It is not unexpected that plants about which so little was actually known and which caused so much confusion and uncertainty should draw upon themselves so rich a store of folklore, superstition and old wives' tales.

The Stinkhorn (Phallus impudicus), the fungus that causes embarrassed giggles whenever the uninitiated see it, seems to have attracted a great deal of interest. This amazing plant, the Latin name of which literally means the unashamed phallus, grows from a round leathery 'egg'. The mature fungus gives off a smell reminiscent of something very dead and this attracts flies from far and wide to come and feast and consequently spread the spores. The eggs were often thought to have come from witches, spirits or devils, no doubt partly because of the appalling stench. Indeed in 1926 the priest of a village in France was set upon by a group of people belonging to a sect called Notre-Dame des Pleurs. They accused him of encouraging certain birds to fly over the garden of the founder of the sect. From the droppings of these birds, it was asserted, came forth obscenely shaped fungi which gave off such vile smells that all those breathing them contracted dire diseases and illnesses.

These fruit bodies were, rather astonishingly, used in ointments for the relief of rheumatism, epilepsy and gout. Whether anyone ever got near enough to the sufferers to find out if the ointment worked is not recorded! Even more surprisingly love potions and aphrodisiacs were also made from the powdered fungus. No doubt the use as an aphrodisiac harks back to the Doctrine of Signatures which held that the shapes and other attributes of plants gave clues to how they could be used medicinally. For example the yellow sap of Greater Celandines (Chelidonium majus) was thought to cure jaundice. Many of the English names of plants describe their uses - Lungwort, Eyebright and Stitchwort being examples. (The suffix 'wort' denoted that the plant was used medicinally).

Needless to say, the Victorians considered stinkhorns to be very unsuitable for women to look upon and the fungus is the subject of a wonderful story about Charles Darwin's eldest

Mushroom or Toadstool?

Is it a mushroom or is it a toadstool? In fact these terms are unique to the English language and really have no precise separate meanings. Traditionally when 'mushroom' is used to describe a fruit body it implies that the fungus is edible whereas 'toadstool' has more sinister overtones suggestive that the fungus is poisonous.

Phallus impudicus

Phallus impudicus
The Stinkhorn

A fungus that usually greets you with it's foul smell long before you see it. The fruit body is egg-shaped and splits open as the white spongy stem expands upwards. The head is covered with a greenish-grey foetid slime which contains the spores. It is very common for much of the year and is eaten in the egg stage by those who believe it to be an aphrodisiac. Egg 2-5cm. Stem 10-20cm. Common.
Edible.

daughter. It seems that this redoubtable lady would arm herself with a pointed stick and a basket and then clad in a special hunting cloak and gloves she would sally forth and track down her prey by sniffing them out. The bodies would then be mortally wounded with the stick and consigned to her basket. The total 'bag' would be brought back to the house and secretly burnt on the drawing room fire - and all this to protect 'the morals of the maids'! The Victorians also ensured that any picture or drawing of this fungus was printed upside down - also, no doubt, to protect delicate sensibilities.

Another fungal manifestation which caused much comment was the so called 'fairy ring'. This phenomenon attracted much speculation and comment and gave rise to many ingenious theories. The most obvious was that the ring of bare earth was caused by the feet of many cavorting fairies who sang as they danced by the light of the moon. The circles thus produced were considered to be magical places, places that

Phallus impudicus

Mutinus caninus

Psathyrella candolleana
Common Psathyrella

This is a delicate little mushroom which grows in groups usually in grass. The bell shaped cap quickly becomes flattened sometimes with remnants of the veil attached at the margin.
Cap 2-6cm. Stem 4-8cm. Common.
Inedible.

Psathyrella hydrophila
Watery Hypholoma

It grows, often in dense tufts, on rotten wood. The cap flattens with age a tawny or dark brown that becomes paler as the toadstool dries out. It often has remnants of veil on the margin.
Cap 2-5cm. Stem 4-10cm. Common.
Edible but worthless.

Psathyrella hydrophila

Mutinus caninus
Dog Stinkhorn

The fruit body starts off as a small 'egg' in the soil from which emerges a pale cream spongy stem with a conical orange head. It grows either solitary, as here, or in groups in the leaf litter of deciduous woods and occasionally conifers. It is fairly common from late summer onwards.
Fruit body 8-12cm high. Occasional.
Inedible.

Psathyrella candolleana

mere mortals entered at their peril. Whereas some believed that the dew from the grass within the circle could be used in love potions or for washing the face on May morning to ensure a beautiful complexion, others warned that to poach this dew for face washing would produce spots and blemishes and to venture into the circle would call down awful retribution.

In Austria the belief was that the circles were caused by dragons whose fiery tails scorched the earth as the dragons flew over. But why these dragons were flying in tiny little circles was not explained! Another suggestion was that the rings were caused by thunder and lightening and yet another that the courting habits of slugs and snails were to blame.

Sadly, reality is far more prosaic. Fairy rings are the result of mycelial growth which radiates out equally in all directions

Clitocybe rivulosa

Clitocybe nebularis

Clitocybe rivulosa
Cracking Clitocybe

This is a dangerous mushroom because it often forms fairy rings in grass in the same way as the edible Marasmius oreades and looks very similar. Great care must be taken because this one is deadly causing muscarine poisoning. Cap 2-5cm. Stem 2-5cm. Common. **Poisonous.**

Clitocybe nebularis
Clouded Agaric

This is a mushroom that is best avoided as many people have developed serious gastric upsets after consuming it. It grows in both deciduous and coniferous woodland usually in rings that can sometimes be so big that it is often difficult to tell that it forms part of a ring at all. The colour ranges from grey to buff and it has a sweet and pleasant smell. Cap 5-20cm. Stem 5-10cm. Common. **Inedible.**

Marasmius oreades
Fairy Ring Champignon

The archetypal fairy ring toadstool. It is very common during the autumn do not confuse this species with Clitocybe rivulosa which looks similar but is deadly poisonous! Cap 2-5cm. Stem 2-8cm. Common. **Edible with reservations.**

Exidia glandulosa

Tremella mesenterica

Exidia glandulosa
Witches Butter

The fruit body is black and jelly like and I suppose just what witches butter would look like. It can be found all the year round on dead wood of broadleaved trees.
(Provided the witches have not been there before you)!
Fruit body 2-5cm. Common.
Inedible.

Tremella mesenterica
Yellow Brain Fungus

A yellow, jelly like fungus folded and convoluted in such a way that it could be said, with some imagination, to resemble a brain. The colour darkens with age and it is found all year on dead deciduous wood especially gorse.
Fruit body 2-8cm. Common.
Inedible.

from a germinating spore. Fruit bodies occur at the periphery of this growth, and as the mycelium advances so it produces chemicals which cause the rings of lush, dark green grass. At the same time, the mycelium on the inside of the circle where the nutrients have been exhausted, dies off and the resulting clogged mass of dead and dying mycelium prevents water from penetrating the soil causing a desert like area. As the dead mycelium finally breaks down so other plants can re-grow and conditions return to normal. Several species grow in rings but probably the best known is Marasmius Oreades the common name of which is 'The Fairy Ring Toadstool'.

Anyone believing in dragons and fairies and other mystic phenomena would have had no trouble at all including witches in the heady brew and several species reflect this. The black, jelly- like Exidia glandulosa delights in the common name Witches Butter. Many people mistakenly use this description for the golden Tremella mesenterica but correctly that should be called Yellow Brain (because of all its folds and convolutions) and anyway, who ever heard of a witch eating anything other than black butter!! 'Witches brooms', those untidy nest-like growths of small twigs found in some trees were also thought to have been the direct result of witches flying past on their broomsticks but quite how this name came about isn't clear. Alas, modern science has mundanely

Daedaleopsis confragosa
Blushing Bracket

A very common and widespread bracket fungus partial to willow whether dead or alive.
The upper surface is usually fawn to russet-brown with a coarse wrinkled texture. The common name derives from the fact that when the off-white pores are bruised they turn or 'blush' a pinky-red.
Fruit body 5-20cm. Common.
Inedible.

Daedaleopsis confragosa

Auricularia mesenterica
Tripe Fungus

This fungus forms folded, gelatinous bracket-like growths on stumps or logs of broadleaved trees especially elm. The upper surface is grey brown, zoned and hairy.
The underside is purplish red often with a white bloom and it can be found growing throughout the year.
Fruit body 2-12cm across. Common.
Inedible.

determined that some of these 'brooms' are caused by the growth of a fungus and others by gall mites. Not nearly so much fun.

In Lapland young men used to seek out a certain fungus (not, one hopes, the stinkhorn) and carry it with them when they went courting. The scent from the fungus was supposed to make them 'more acceptable' to their chosen young ladies. Certainly more original than red roses, and presumably a forerunner of aftershave!

The Fly Agaric

The toadstool which has undoubtedly excited more attention and produced more stories than any other is the Fly Agaric *(Amanita muscaria)*. This is the archetypal toadstool and is enchantingly pretty with its red cap thickly sprinkled with white, mealy flecks. It is beloved by all from fairytale aficionados and devotees of Beatrix Potter to artists and photographers the world over. The latter like to portray the toadstool being daintily nibbled by mice, hedgehogs or squirrels or providing a seat or shelter for a variety of creatures from fairies to frogs. But behind the innocent facade lies a darkly powerful and sinister character. For this toadstool is one of the band of hallucinogenic fungi; it is also extremely poisonous and experimentation is not to be recommended.

Most hallucinogenic or 'magic' mushrooms are small, brown and inconspicuous but let it be said that not all small, brown and inconspicuous toadstools are hallucinogenic. Some, particularly those belonging to the Inocybe family are deadly poisonous and misidentification could lead to a painful death.

Nothing much could be confused with the Fly Agaric except possibly 'The Sickener' *(Russula emetica)*, a toadstool which belongs to a completely different genus and which

Amanita muscaria
Fly Agaric

Without doubt the best known toadstool beloved by artists and photographers alike. The bright scarlet cap is covered in distinctive white mealy flecks which are often washed off by the rain leaving the cap smooth often with the colour faded. It forms an association with birch and appears from late summer to late autumn. Cap 8-20cm. Stem 8-20cm. Common.
Poisonous.

Amanita muscaria

Amanita muscaria

Amanita muscaria

superficially resembles a Fly Agaric with the spots washed off. This toadstool as its name suggests will cause violent stomach upsets if eaten raw.

The Fly Agaric gets its name from a practice which used to be common in Europe. A saucer of milk was laced with pieces of the said toadstool and in theory this produced a lethal brew which flies avidly drank and subsequently died. However, it has now been proved that flies which collapse after drinking this mixture are not actually dead, but stoned out of their minds and given time they will recover and come back for more.

Another myth involves the Vikings who supposedly ate Fly Agarics before going into battle. This was thought to be the cause of their extremely violent behaviour. However, once again modern science, no lover of romantic ideas, has exploded the theory and sadly it is now known that had the Vikings really eaten this fungus they would have become pussycats rather than raging lions and would have wanted to do nothing more strenuous than curl up and enjoy their vivid dreams.

One good reason for not experimenting with the Fly Agaric is the fact that it is poisonous. It used to be considered deadly but technology has succeeded in isolating and identifying

Amanita muscaria

Amanita muscaria

Russula mairei
Beechwood Sickener

Very similar to Russula emetica although the cap tends to be velvety. Once again the gills and stem are white, the gills turning cream with age. As you can see here and as the common names indicates it grows, often in groups, in beechwoods.
Cap 5-10cm. Stem 2-5cm. Common.
Poisonous.

Russula mairei

Russula emetica

Russula emetica
The Sickener

Clearly one of the most beautiful of the Russulas with its scarlet cap contrasting with the pure white stem and gills. When wet the cap becomes viscid (sticky) and the margin tends to be lined as the fungus matures. Said by some to smell of coconut it is mainly found growing amongst conifers often in moss.
Cap 3-10cm. Stem 4-9cm. Common.
Poisonous.

many of the poisons the plant contains and although we now know it is not usually fatal it can nevertheless make life very unpleasant. Few deaths have been directly attributed to the Fly Agaric but one which concerned Count de Vecchi who was a member of the Italian Diplomatic Corps in the USA in 1893. He ate 24 Fly Agarics for breakfast one morning and, after suffering 'violent convulsions' died the next day.

It was from Siberia and Lapland that most of the stories concerning this toadstool came. Travellers would tell of tribes, particularly the Koryaks and Kamchadals for whom the Fly Agaric equated to 'the *haschish* and *majoon* of the East.' These tribes would gather the toadstools and dry them as this is said to increase the narcotic properties. Some tribes, displaying extreme male chauvinist tendencies, gave the women the job of chewing the fungi first thus eliminating most of the poisons. The men then took charge and enjoyed the hallucinogenic left-overs in comparative safety. It is recorded time and again that not only do the toadstools have hallucinogenic qualities but so too does the urine of anyone who has eaten them. And one account tells us that even the fifth distillation is still effective.

According to an account by Wasson (a well known expert on the folkore of fungi), reindeer too were addicted to both Fly Agarics and human urine and when either was nearby would 'become unmanageable'. The same account goes on to say 'Reindeer, like men, suffer (or enjoy) profound mental disturbances after eating Fly Agaric'. When a drunken animal was found, it would be killed and the flesh eaten because that too would be intoxicating! One wonders if these stories

Russula atropurpurea
Blackish-Purple Russula

Like many of the russulas the cap colour is very variable, in this species from purplish-red to black contrasted by white gills and stem. It grows from late summer in mixed woodland especially under oak. The flesh has a fruity, some say apple, smell when bruised and tastes somewhat peppery. Cap 2-4cm. Stem 4-8cm. Common.
Inedible.

Russula queletii

Russula queletii

The cap varies from purple to a rich wine red and the stem colour matches. It is found in coniferous woods. Cap 4-10cm. Stem 2-8cm. Uncommon. **Inedible.**

Russula atropurpurea

Russula vesca

Russula vesca
Bare Toothed Russula

The English name refers to the fact that the cap cuticle does not quite reach the margin and thus leaves the ends of the gills exposed. It can be found in deciduous woodland from late spring. Cap 5-10cm. Stem 3-10cm. Common. **Edible.**

Sparassis crispa
Cauliflower Fungus

Really the fruit body looks more like a sponge than the head of a cauliflower. The surface is pale beige to cream and consists of intricately folded and furrowed lobes that unfortunately provide good hiding places for insects.

As a consequence it needs to be thoroughly washed and inspected before it can be safely eaten. It grows from a short thick stem that is often buried. It is specifically parasitic on conifer trees, mainly pine in Britain, appearing during late summer onwards. Fruit body 5-50cm. Fairly common.
Edible and good.

Sparassis crispa

Stropharia aeruginosa

Stropharia aeruginosa
Verdigris Agaric

A common little toadstool that can be found in almost any habitat growing on the soil. Its striking blue-green colour comes from the gluten which covers the cap, in fact if this is washed off by rain then the true cap colour of pale yellow is revealed. Two very noticeable features are the white scales which float in the gluten and adhere to the margin and a white stem covered in very obvious floccose (cottony) scales. Cap 4-8cm Stem 3-6cm. Common. **Inedible.**

provide the source of the myth of Father Christmas and his flying reindeer. But the fact remains that despite all its weird and wonderful effects the Fly Agaric is poisonous and it is not alone. There are other toadstools which, if eaten, quite simply kill.

Although Britain was considered by some to be 'le pays plus mycophobe du globe' there are reasons to think that many people in this country did enjoy eating mushrooms, at least in mediaeval times and that the fear and distrust of them only arose later. There is no doubt whatsoever that the Romans and Greeks were avid consumers of fungi - rich men employed collectors and special pots were used for cooking these delicacies. Equally there is no doubt that the same Greeks and Romans were very adept in dispatching their enemies with a dish of edible mushrooms laced with deadly ones or, alternatively, spiking drinks with juice from poisonous toadstools. There have been, and still are, many deaths from poisoning on the Continent, mainly of people who confuse the Death Cap (*Amanita phalloides*) with edible species.

It is true that there are more edible species than poisonous ones and the really deadly species are few in number. However, the only way to be absolutely sure that you are not about to wipe yourself off the face of the earth is to know your toadstools and be able to confidently identify them. Either that, or get to know an 'expert' and ask them. In Europe most towns or cities have at least one Pharmacy where avid

Amanita phalloïdes

Amanita phalloides

Amanita phalloides
Death Cap

This one of the most deadly toadstools in the world responsible for more deaths than any other species. Despite its sinister nature it is quite attractive with its olive green cap (also white or grey). The surface is smooth with no veil remnants and it grows from a bulbous and noticably ragged volva. The stem is white and sometimes has a snake-like banding. It is common and widespread growing in deciduous woodland especially under oak and beech. Cap 5-12cm. Stem 5-15cm. Common.
Poisonous and deadly.

mycophagists can go with the booty they have collected to have it identified.

Many toadstools look superficially very alike and mistakes are easily made. Don't for one minute believe any of the old wives' tales because not one has any truth in it…

'Edible toadstools peel, poisonous ones don't'.

'Contact with poisonous fungi when they are being cooked will turn silver black.'

'Cook pears with poisonous toadstools and the pears will remove all the poisons.'

'Fungi eaten by slugs, rabbits or squirrels are safe for humans to eat.'

No, no, no and no. John Ramsbottom in his book Mushrooms and Toadstools says that 'The only certain test is eating.' But

Amanita echinocephala

Amanita citrina

Amanita fulva

Amanita fulva
Tawny Grisette

A common and widespread member of the Amanita family found in a variety of habitats. It appears from a sac-like bag called a volva and clearly this specimen has carried part of the universal veil with it on the cap. The universal veil is the protective covering that encloses the mushroom at the 'egg' stage whilst in the soil. Cap 4-10cm. Stem 10-20cm. Common. **Edible when cooked.**

Amanita echinocephala

This rare amanita prefers to grow on dry chalky soils usually amongst scrub or tree cover. I found this one under beech on downland in Southern England, where the species regularly appears from July-September. Cap 5-18cm. Stem 5-15cm. Rare. **Poisonous.**

Amanita citrina
False Death Cap

A common and widespread mushroom which grows on the ground in broad-leaved and mixed woodlands especially those containing beech. It appears singly or in small groups from the summer onwards. The fact that it can easily be confused with the deadly Amanitas like phalloides and virosa makes this one best left alone. One important distinguishing feature of the flesh is that, when crushed, it smells of raw potatoes. Cap 5-15cm. Stem 5-10cm. Common. **Edible but unpalatable and best avoided.**

Amanita spissa

Amanita spissa

The stem is white above a striate (fine lined) ring and greyish below. It is a common and widespread mushroom found mainly in conifer woodland. Although edible (when thoroughly cooked) it lacks any real taste and is best avoided because of its similarity to A. pantherina. Cap 8-15cm. Stem 5-15cm. Common. **Edible with reservations.**

Amanita pantherina
Panther Cap

An uncommon species which can be recognised by the brown cap with white scales. The white flesh lacks a distinctive smell and, unlike A. rubescens, does not turn red when bruised. It can be found mainly in deciduous woodland from July onwards. Cap 5-15cm. Stem 5-12cm. Uncommon. **Extremely poisonous.**

Amanita rubescens
The Blusher

The cap is a pale reddish-brown and covered with greyish mealy remnants of the veil. The most important diagnostic feature of this fungus is that the flesh will flush pink, (hence blusher), when bruised or eaten by slugs. It is edible but only if thoroughly cooked. Cap 8-18cm. Stem 5-15cm. Very common. **Edible with reservations.**

Amanita pantherina

Amanita rubescens

Armillaria mellea

how many amateur mycologists would be willing to be sacrificed in the name of scientific discovery? Perhaps we should reiterate that the only way to be safe is to learn to identify and in particular learn to identify the Amanita genus which contains so many of the deadly toadstools.

So what exactly are these toadstools? They are the visible fruiting bodies of an organism, the main food gathering part of which is the mycelium or root system. One of the peculiarities of toadstools is that they do not contain any chlorophyll and therefore are unable to photosynthesise, that is, make use of the energy from sunlight as do most plants. Consequently they have to obtain the necessary nutrients from plant and animal material. Saprophytic fungi are those which live on dead or dying matter, helping to break it down and release chemicals back into the soil. The more sinister parasitic fungi invade live material often causing enormous damage and, in some cases, killing off their host. Good examples of this are the well known Honey Fungus *(Armillaria mellea)*, every gardener's nightmare, and Cordyceps militaris, the fruit bodies of which look like little red matchsticks, which parasitises beetle larvae and caterpillars living beneath the soil.

Armillaria mellea
Honey Fungus

This is both a parasitic and saprophytic fungus that will infect most trees and shrubs eventually causing the death of its host. A feature of this fungus is the long black rhizomorphs known as "bootlaces" which occur under the bark and are capable of travelling long distances under the soil in search of a new host. It is edible when cooked although it can cause stomach upsets with some people. Cap 4-16cm. Stem 4-16cm. Common.
Edible with reservations.

Armillaria mellea

Orobanche rapum-genistae
Greater Broomrape

The flowers of the parasitic broomrapes look very similar to those of orchids but they are most closely related to foxgloves. They are relatively easy to identify as they are host specific thus the knapweed broomrape only grows on knapweed, the ivy broomrape only grows on ivy, etc.

Orobanche rapum-genistae

Some fungi are both parasitic and saprophytic in that once they have killed a plant they will continue to feed on the dead remains. Fungi belong in the group of decomposers and play a vital role in the food chain and the cycle of life and death.

It is interesting to note that there are a few flowering plants which also do not contain chlorophyll, most notably the Broomrapes which parasitise a variety of plants including Yarrow, Ivy, Thyme and Knapweed; and the saprophytic Birds Nest Orchid which is found in woodland and gets its nutrients from the surrounding leaf mould.

Classification

All plants and animals are classified into Kingdoms. The Kingdom Fungi is split into Divisions then into sub-divisions

Neottia nidus-avis
Bird's Nest Orchid

The bird's nest orchid is a saprophyte and grows on the decaying leaves in beechwoods. It has thick branching roots that resemble a bird's nest which are incapable of obtaining nutrition from the soil directly, in fact they only survive by an association with a fungus that grows on the rotting leaves.
This association is known as a mycorrhizal association.

Lathraea squamaria

Lathraea squamaria
Toothwort

Toothwort parasitises the roots of trees such as elm and, as here, hazel. It derives its common name from the fact that in the middle ages it was used as a cure for toothache.

Neottia nidus-avis

then Classes then Orders then Genera and finally the specific names. It is these last two, the generic and specific names, that we will be mostly concerned with here.

Nomenclature

Confusion of a different kind is still rife today however. This arises over the words mushroom, toadstool and fungus and the delicate question of when to correctly use each one or whether they are interchangeable. This problem is not helped by pronouncements such as the one in the 'Grete Herball' of 1526 which says 'Fungi ben mussherons...there be two manners of them one manner is deedly and sleeth them that eateth of them and be called tode stoles, and the other doeth not.' From the north country comes the useful 'mushrooms as is toadstools'.

Some consider that the word mushroom should be used for all edible species and toadstool for the rest but this immediately leads to problems such as what to do with species that are described as 'edibility unknown' or, even more tersely, 'not edible'. Another suggestion is that they should all be known as toadstools and the word mushroom should be used specifically for one group or genus, namely Agaricus, which contains the

Woodland in Autumn, Sussex, England.

field, wood and horse mushrooms. However, even the experts don't seem able to agree on this one, and broadly speaking the two words are interchangeable and could perhaps be equated to the words 'flowers and weeds'. The field is open for personal interpretation. When in doubt, the words fungus or fungi usefully cover everything.

The derivations of the words are interesting too. Mushroom is thought to come from the French mousseron (mousse meaning moss). Toadstool could have come from words such as todestole (1300s), toadstooles, paddockstooles and toody's hatte. But an alternative suggestion points to the German word tode meaning death. Whatever the truth may be, there is no doubt that toadstools were considered to be formed from 'the harmful substances of the earth and the venom of toads'. Add to this the fact that they were found in dark, damp places where toads lurk and the association is complete. Fungus is widely supposed to come from the Greek Sphonggos meaning a sponge but another derivation which initially came from Bauhin in 1650 and which appealed to many is funus - a funeral and ago - I lead (or go) to.

Piptoporus betulinus
Birch Bracket or Razor Strop

A smooth thick shell-shaped bracket fungus, pale grey brown to buff with white pores discolouring with age. This fungus grows exclusively on birch trees and has had many uses in the past including being used as corn plasters and as a strop for the old fashioned cut-throat razors. Fruit body 5-20cm. Common.
Inedible.

Piptoporus betulinus

Fomes fomentarius

Fomes fomentarius
Hoof or Tinder Fungus

This hoof shaped bracket fungus persists on the tree for many years and can attain a size in excess of 50cm across and 25cm high.
I have only found this species on four occasions in southern England, each time growing on beech. In Scotland, however, it is very common, on a recent trip I found it on virtually every birch tree I looked at! Fruit body 10-50cm. Extremely rare in England.
Inedible.

Identification

As stated earlier, this is not a technical book and therefore the question of identification is approached from a general point of view.

First of all, note where the toadstool is growing. Is it in woodland, grassland or the middle of a city pavement. If it's woodland, then what sort of woodland - coniferous, broadleaved or mixed and is the fungus growing on wood or in the soil. If on wood, is the wood living or dead? What sort of trees are in the vicinity - Oak, Ash, Birch, Beech, etc. This is important as some toadstools will only grow near certain types of tree. For example, the Death Cap is almost always found near Oak or Beech. In Britain the Fly Agaric favours Birch and Pine. The reason for this is that certain species of toadstool have what is known as a mycorrhizal association with certain species of trees and this association is mutually beneficial, each helping the other to obtain vital nutrients in

Phellinus igniarius
False Tinder Fungus

A thick, hard and corky fungus that is initially grey but gets darker, almost black, with age. It is often hoof-shaped, wrinkled and furrowed on the upper surface which often cracks with age. It grows on deciduous trees with a preference for willow in which it causes heart rot. Here we see a spectacular specimen that has given rise to the many smaller fruit bodies.
Fruit body 5-20cm. Common.
Inedible.

Ganoderma resinaceum

Ganoderma adspersum

Ganoderma applanatum
Artist's Fungus

*A semi-circular bracket which is greyish-brown to dark chocolate brown with an upper surface that is hard, grooved and knobbly. It can be found growing solitary or in overlapping tiers with the result that the lower brackets will often be covered by a layer of cocoa coloured spores. It is found all the year round on living or dead deciduous trees, especially beech in which it causes white rot. Fruit body 10-40cm. Uncommon. **Inedible.***

Ganoderma adspersum** is virtually identical in habit and appearance but is more common. The main distinguishing feature is that the dark brown flesh does not have the white flecking found in G. applanatum. **Inedible.

Ganoderma resinaceum
Lacquered Bracket

*This is a rare and very impressive bracket fungus with an upper surface that looks as though it has been varnished. It is a long-lived fungus that can be found throughout the year growing on living and dead deciduous trees, particularly oak in which it causes a serious heart rot. I am indebted to Ted Green of the British Mycological Society and a passionate mushroom conservationist, for showing me this magnificent specimen growing in Windsor Great Park. Fruit body 10-60cm. Rare. **Inedible.***

Ganoderma applanatum

Laetiporus sulphureus

Laetiporus sulphureus
Chicken of the Woods

Unfortunately this beautiful and striking fungus marks the beginning of the end for its host trees as it causes rot in the heart wood, turning it into a crumbling brown mass. It is a common fungus found worldwide and in Britain grows on living trees such as oak, willow, chestnut and yew. I took these pictures in a yew forest in southern England where I found virtually every other tree had the fungus in it. Many of the fruit bodies were damaged by a resident herd of fallow deer, but this magnificent specimen was growing way above their browse line and, as a consequence, in perfect condition. The fungus is edible, particularly when young, provided that it is soaked in water first which effectively removes the sour taste. Below a superb specimen growing on oak. Fruit body 10-40cm across. 10-60cm high. Common.
Edible - but with reservations.

the shape of water or mineral salts. This association is called a symbiotic relationship.

Now take note of the toadstool itself and look for distinguishing features. The most obvious will probably be the cap colour but look also at the texture of the cap. Is there a ring on the stem and does the stem grow out of a volva or sac-like structure. Is there anything adhering to the cap in the form of flecks of mealy material or cobwebby particles. Then look under the cap and note whether there are gills, pores or teeth or a smooth leathery surface (more likely to be found in some bracket fungi). Note the colour of the gills (or pores or teeth) and, if possible, check the colour of the spores. By now you will probably have picked the toadstool so sniff it and see whether there are any distinguishing smells. Many toadstools are blessed with strong smells such as camphor, coconut, curry, aniseed, garlic and raw potatoes.

Laetiporus sulphureus

Certain species such as Russula and Lactarius can be tasted - a very small portion of the cap can be nibbled and then spat out - but don't try this until you can confidently distinguish the different species. Always be guided by the maxim 'When in doubt, throw it out' and remember the saying 'There are old

Hericium erinaceus

Hericium erinaceus

Hericium erinaceus
Bearded Tooth Fungus

Late on Sunday evening I received a telephone call from my good friend Doris Ashby telling me that one of these amazing fruit bodies had appeared in the New Forest. Despite having photographed it herself she was quite prepared to go back again so that I could photograph if for this book. We arrived early the following morning only to discover that it was no longer on the tree. It had been taken, in all probability, by the commercial mushroom collectors that have become the scourge of this area in recent years.
Finally, as these photographs show, I was successful following a further two trips to other locations in the New Forest, clocking up a total of 800 miles in the process. Imagine my frustration when just two weeks later, I was to see three more fruit bodies growing less than 30 miles from my home.

Hericium coralloides
Coral Spine Fungus

A truly beautiful and stunning fungus reminiscent of a piece of coral. I cannot describe the sheer joy on seeing this fungus for the very first time. The fruit body consists of a solid mass growing on the wood, the outer surface made up of many creamy-white coral like branches. It grows mainly on beech during early autumn and in Britain is extremely rare. As such it deserves protection and on no account should it be picked.

mushroom hunters and bold mushrooms hunters but there are no old, bold mushroom hunters'. To the uninitiated these precautions probably seem to be verging on the hysterical but look more closely at some of the deadly toadstools and the reasons for such caution become apparent.

Hericium Coralloides

Inonotus dryadeus

This is a large, irregularly shaped bracket fungus that can be found growing from late summer through to autumn at the base of oak trees. I have also found it on birch, alder and, as here, on beech. This stage in its growth is the one I consider to be the best and most spectacular. Here the young fruit body is characteristically 'weeping' reminding me of the old fashioned honeycomb. Fruit body 10-50cm. Uncommon.
Inedible.

Poisonous Fungi

The poisonous fungi are very often grouped according to the poisons they contain and the effects these produce on human beings. The five most commonly accepted categories are:

Cellular or cytolytic poisoning The toadstools in this group are responsible for the more severe cases of poisoning. The poisons attack the organs of the body and cause degeneration and breakdown.

Nerve poisoning Here substances such as muscarine and ibotenic acid are involved and the nervous system is affected. Species such as Inocybe and Clitocybe contain these poisons.

Gastric poisoning Many of the poisonous mushrooms are found in this group. The seriousness of the poisoning can be governed by the age and condition of the fungus and the sensitivity of the person involved. Species such as the Yellow Staining Mushroom (*Agaricus xanthodermus*); Fairy Cakes (*Hebeloma crustuliniforme*); Devil's Boletus (*Boletus satanus*)

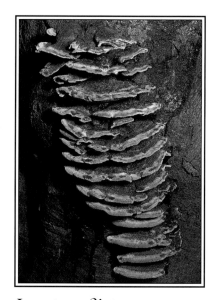

Inonotus radiatus

Inonotus radiatus
Alderwood Polypore

A small brown woody polypore usually forming several uneven tiered brackets. Gradually the colour changes from brown to black with a paler margin and it can be found growing on broadleaved trees, especially alder where it causes serious rot. Fruit body 3-8cm. Common. **Inedible.**

Grifola frondosa

Polyporus squamosus
Dryad's Saddle

This fungus often forms quite large columns of overlapping yellowish caps which are covered with dark brown scales. It grows from late spring to early autumn on trunks of deciduous trees especially beech usually as a wound parasite. Fruit body 5-60cm. Stem 5-10cm. Common.
Edible when young.

Polyporus squamosus

Fistulina hepatica

Fistulina hepatica
Beefsteak Fungus

The fruit body of this fungus initially appears as a cushion which then grows into a tongue-shaped bracket. The flesh, if cut, is red and moist resembling raw steak. Unfortunately the similarity ends here for although widely eaten it is very acidic and lacking in flavour. Fruit body 10-25cm. Common.
Edible.

Grifola frondosa
Hen of the Woods

I think you will agree with me the fruit body is really stunning and certainly photogenic especially when, like this specimen, it is in pristine condition. This is a parasitic fungus found in the autumn growing at the base of living deciduous trees particularly beech and oak. Unfortunately it smells awful, an odour said by some to be reminiscent of house mice! Fruit body 15-40cm high. Uncommon.
Edible.

and Sulphur Tuft *(Hypholoma fasiculare)* are all included in this group, along with many others.

Hallucinogenic poisoning This has already been mentioned. The toadstools in this group contain psilocybin and are usually small and often brown. Species known to contain this poison include Psilocybe, Conocybe, Stropharia and Panaeolus. They are easily confused with the smaller members of the genus Lepiota some of which are deadly poisonous.

Alcohol and Toadstools One species in particular is involved here namely the Common Ink Cap *(Coprinus atramentarius)*. At first sight similar in appearance to the Shaggy Ink Cap, which of course is edible, this species contains Coprine which is activated when eaten in conjunction with alcohol. The effects

Meripilus giganteus

are identical to those induced by the drug Antabuse which is used in the treatment of alcoholism. The symptoms are flushing of the face, rapid pulse, sweating, nausea, headache and mental confusion. these symptoms can last for several hours and reappear if alcohol is consumed again during the next few days. Other species implicated in this group include two from the Clitocybe genus.

The genus Amanita contains several species which are either deadly or can cause great discomfort and illness. For this reason, although there are one or two species which are edible, it is advisable to leave the Amanitas out of any proposed culinary experiments. Nearly all the Amanitas have a volva or sac at the base and a soft floppy ring on the stem. Depending on the texture of the cap, some have blotches of material adhering to the top of the cap.

The best known, certainly the most publicised and feared species is the Death Cap *(Amanita phalloides)*. Misleadingly this is a very attractive plant with its olive green cap (the colour can vary and more unusually, can be grey or white)

Meripilus giganteus
Giant Polypore

This is a formidable fungus that grows at the base of beech trees and occasionally oak. Sometimes it will appear in the soil several metres from the trunk but in reality it is firmly attached to a root. Numerous fan shaped caps arise from a central base, and vary in colour from yellowish grey to buff. This fungus is common and widespread appearing any time from late summer through to the first frosts whereupon it turns black and dies. Fruit body 20-40cm. Common.
Inedible.

Meripilus giganteus

Tyromyces lacteus

Tyromyces lacteus
Milk-White Polypore

*The fruit body is fan shaped,
creamy white and faintly zoned with
similarly coloured pores that darken
with age. It is found mainly on
deciduous wood.
Fruit body 2-8cm. Common.*
Inedible.

Phaeolus schweinitzii
Large Pine Polypore

*A large velvety, bracket shaped
fungus at first dark yellow becoming
purplish brown with a paler yellow
margin. It is supported by a short
tough brown stem and grows low
down on pine trees which it
parasitises causing serious heart rot.
Fruit body 10-20cm. Stem 2-6cm.
Fairly common.*
Inedible.

Polyporus badius
Bay Polypore

*The chestnut brown cap, which has a
darker centre, is funnel shaped and
wrinkled. It grows on a black velvety
stem usually on the dead wood of
deciduous trees from spring onwards.
Cap 5-20cm. Stem 2-8cm. Rare.*
Inedible.

Phaeolus schweinitzii

Xylaria polymorpha

and creamy white gills. there is a ring on the stem and the volva is large and ragged edged. One medium sized cap of this toadstool could kill at least four people. The effects of the poisons, the most virulent of which are the amatoxins, do not show up for several hours after the toadstool has been eaten. Vomiting, diarrhoea and dehydration are among the symptoms. There follows a remission period of anything up to three days after which the original symptoms return and, as massive damage has been caused to the liver and kidneys, death follows.

Other species which also contain these poisons include some of the Lepiota genus and some of the Galerinas. This underlines the need for identification skills on the part of the would be gourmet as some members of the Lepiota group are edible and good, and Galerinas are small and golden brown and could easily be confused with some of the hallucinogenic toadstools.

A species which is considered by some to be edible is the Turk's Cap or Turban fungus *(Gyromitra esculenta)*. Given the specific name of esculenta, one would expect the plant to be edible and in some Scandinavian countries it is eaten as it is

Xylaria polymorpha
Dead Man's Fingers

It strikes me that this fungus must have been given its ghoulish common name at a time when most people were actually aware of what dead men's fingers looked like!
The black fruit body is club shaped with a rough uneven surface. It grows on the dead wood of deciduous trees throughout the year.
Fruit body 3-8cm. Common.
Inedible.

Bulgaria inquinans
Black Bulgar

A common species that grows clustered on dead trunks of deciduous trees especially oak. The black fruit bodies have a tough rubbery texture and are at first cup shaped later becoming flattened. It can be found from autumn to winter.
Fruit body 1-4cm. Common.
Inedible.

Daldinia concentrica

Daldinia concentrica
King Alfred's Cakes
or Cramp Balls

*A common fungus that grows
gregariously on dead wood especially
ash and beech. The hard black or
dark brown fruit bodies at one time
were carried by country folk to ward
off the effects of cramp. This fungus
has the option of two English
common names which can cause
embarrassment if mixed up!
Fruit body 2-5cm. Common.*
Inedible.

Xylaria hypoxylon
Stagshorn
or Candle Snuff Fungus

*The fruit body is branched and
reminiscent of antlers. These
branches are black with white tips
but become totally black as the fruit
body matures. It is common and
widespread being found on dead wood
all the year round.
Fruit body 1-6cm. Common.*
Inedible.

Xylaria hypoxylon

Merulius tremellosus

Merulius tremellosus
Jelly Rot Fungus

The upper surface of these narrow overlapping brackets are covered in silky hair-like fibres, coloured creamy-white on top and salmon pink to orange below. The fruit body is soft and flabby and grows on the undersides of the dead wood of deciduous trees from autumn through to spring.
Brackets 1-5cm. Occasional.
Inedible.

said to be safe once dried after it has been boiled in water for at least ten minutes at a temperature of 87° C. The water then has to be thrown away and the fungus re-boiled. However, recent research has discovered that the fungus contains powerful carcinogens as well as the chemical monomethylhydrazine (one of the components of rocket fuel)! The poisons, including Gyromitrin, attack the central nervous system and cause nausea, vomiting, cramps, convulsions and coma.

Paxillus involutus or the Brown Roll Rim is another species which is apparently edible after cooking. However, the poisons it contains seem to be cumulative and repeated eating of this fungus can lead to fatalities.

The Cortinarius genus contains several very toxic species. Probably the most deadly are *Cortinarius orellanus* and *Cortinarius speciosissimus* both of which contain orellanin. One of the most sinister aspects of this kind of poisoning is that there is a period of anything between two and fourteen days before the effects of the poisons become apparent (a useful fact for the writers of detective fiction)! The main organs to be afflicted are the kidneys although there may be damage to

Morchella esculenta

Morchella esculenta
Common Morel

The head of the fruit body resembles a brown sponge with irregular pits and ridges. The overall colour is a yellow-brown that darkens as the fungus matures. It grows on a creamy-white brittle stem in a variety of habitats during the spring.
Fruit body 5-20cm high. Rare.
Edible and good.

Morchella semilibera
Half-Free Morel

I was told, rather belatedly, where these rare morels were growing on the south downs in Sussex. Unfortunately, on my arrival it was obvious that I was too late, they had gone over and the few that were still standing were not worth photographing. I decided to search the surrounding slopes desperate to find a half decent specimen but without any confidence. Imagine my delight when in less than fifteen minutes I found this one, not only perfect but growing alongside a dog violet that makes the picture both pictorial and informative.
Cap 2-5cm. Stem 10-20cm. Rare.
Edible.

Gyromitra esculenta

Gyromitra esculenta
False Morel

This strange looking fungus with its lobes and convolutions resembling a miniature brain is quite rare in Britain. It grows in association with conifers particularly pine during the spring. The cap is a reddish-brown that sometimes grows downwards concealing a short delicate white stem. Although the name Esculenta means 'edible' it is extremely poisonous and has been responsible for many deaths. The poison is destroyed by cooking but there is some evidence that it can accumulate in the body with dire consequences.
Cap 5-15cm. Rare.
Poisonous and deadly.

Morchella semilibera

Helvella crispa

Helvella elastica

Helvellas

Helvella crispa *appears anytime from late summer growing (either singly or in troops) on the ground in woodlands, parks and roadside verges. The cap is convoluted, lobed and commonly described as saddle-shaped. The cylindrical stem is hollow with a ribbed outer surface that resembles a stick of celery.* ***Helvella lacunosa*** *appears at the same time and is very similar to H. crispa except that it's colour is grey through to black, crispa is always creamy-white.* ***Helvella elastica*** *differs markedly from the other two by virtue of the smooth white stem topped with a brown cap. All three are poisonous unless thoroughly cooked but this process renders them virtually worthless.* ***All are poisonous.***

Helvella lacunosa

the liver and nervous system as well. Of three adults who collected and ate this fungus in Scotland a few years ago, two required kidney transplants to save their lives.

The last entrant in the poisonous category must be Ergot (*Claviceps purpurea*). This remarkable fungus which infects grasses and grain was responsible in the Middle Ages for outbreaks of a terrible disease which came to be known as St. Anthony's Fire. Sufferers were either afflicted with a sensation known as 'formication' (a feeling that ants are running about under the skin) and a burning in their limbs which then became swollen. In severe cases fingers, toes and even arms and legs would wither and had to be amputated.

Alternatively, the minds of the victims were attacked and

Hydnum repandum

Cantharellus cibarius

Hygrophoropsis aurantiaca

Hydnum repandum
The Hedgehog Fungus

The cap of this lovely little toadstool is coloured ochre-buff on a velvety upper surface. Turn it over and instead of gills or pores you will find crowded, creamy-white spines. The stem is white and stout. It grows in both coniferous and broadleaved woodlands. Cap 3-10cm. Stem 2-6cm. **Edible and good.**

Cantharellus cibarius
The Chanterelle

This is a much sought after edible mushroom with a superb flavour. It grows either solitary, as shown, or in troops favouring acid soils in mixed woodlands from late summer to autumn. It has a sour taste if eaten raw and a very distinctive smell of apricots which is one of the features that separates it from the false chanterelle. Cap 2-10cm. Stem 2-8cm. Common. **Edible excellent.**

Craterellus cornucopiodes

Craterellus cornucopiodes
Horn of Plenty or
Trompet du Mort

They often grow in profusion especially on calcareous soils under beech. Fruit body 5-10cm. Common.
Edible and good.

Hygrophoropsis aurantiaca
The False Chanterelle

It is often confused with the real chanterelle but this pretty little toadstool is much more orange in colour and the gills are more regular and deeper orange than those of Cantharellus cibarius. This species is usually associated with pine woods and heathlands from late summer through to autumn.
Cap 2-8cm. Stem 2-6cm. Common.
Edible but known to produce hallucinations!

violent convulsions, hallucinations and manic behaviour resulted. This poisoning was more common in Europe where Rye bread played an important part in the daily diet. One particularly bad outbreak in France in 944 AD is said to have killed more than 40,000 people.

As there was, at that time, no scientific understanding of the causes for these sudden outbreaks of madness and death, it is not surprising that people began to believe they were caused by witchcraft and devils - or that it was a sort of divine retribution for sins committed.

St Anthony came to be connected with the disease because he was reputed to protect people from fire and epilepsy. His remains were buried at Dauphine and many made pilgrimages to this town in the hope of a cure. Not surprisingly hundreds of 'miracles' took place possibly because once the sufferers were removed from their usual food supply, the symptoms were mitigated.

Ergot having now been tamed by science, provides valuable

Collybia butyracea
The Butter Cap

The cap colour is very variable from a dark reddish-brown to buff and the flesh feels greasy to the touch hence the English name. It grows in the leaf litter under trees from Autumn onwards. Cap 2-8cm. Stem 5-10cm. Occasional. **Edible.**

Collybia confluens

Collybia confluens
Clustered Tough-Shank

A common member of the **Collybia** *family which is represented by almost 40 species in Britain. This one grows in quite large tufts in the leaf litter of deciduous woodlands. Cap 3-5cm. Stem 3-5cm. Common.* **Edible.**

Craterellus cornucopiodes
Horn of Plenty or
Trompet du Mort

It is so easy to walk past these funnel shaped fungi and not see them even though they often grow in profusion especially on calcareous soils under beech. The colour can vary from jet black to grey or brownish-grey. They are common and widespread, the best time to look for them is following a period of rain in the autumn. Fruit body 5-10cm. Common. **Edible and good.**

Collybia butyracea

drugs which are used particularly to alleviate the symptoms of migraine and in obstetrics to facilitate childbirth.

When it comes to conservation, an emotive and complex subject, fungi are not the first things that spring to mind. Rather it is the obvious - the birds, flowers, insects, animals and trees which attract attention and sympathy. But fungi are a part of the overall picture, an important part, and fungi are vulnerable and threatened too.

For many years, indeed until the advent of the train and then the car, people from the towns did not venture much into the countryside. Local people used fruits, berries and wild plants for food but took only what they required. Today the countryside has come to represent recreation and a source to be plundered, a wild area to be tamed and suburbanised.

Xerocomus badius

Xerocomus badius
The Bay Boletus

This boletus is often confused by beginners with the Penny Bun B. edulis but it lacks the reticulation (netting) on the stem and secondly the pores of edulis do not turn blue when bruised. It is a widespread and common mushroom appearing from late Summer onwards in a variety of habitats. The cap when dry is felty in appearance but becomes viscid when wet, the pores are pale olive-yellow. Cap 5-10cm. Stem 5-10cm. Common. **Edible.**

Boletus edulis

Very few people see themselves as an integral part of the food chain and the web of interdependence. Most seem to think that they stand outside 'nature' and that it is there for their convenience and entertainment. With an ever increasing population, improved travel, access to the countryside made easier and encouragement of activities like mountain biking and 4-wheel drive clubs, our wildlife is now seriously under threat and sadly this includes, in no small way, our fungi.

Many people say that because fungi produce so many spores, picking the fruit body does no harm. But before a spore can germinate it needs exactly the right conditions and consequently millions perish. Assuming that a spore does find the ideal place, it germinates and sends out a thread like

Boletus edulis
The Penny Bun or Cep

Common in all woodlands but with a clear preference for beech and oak, this is probably the best known member of the boletus family. It is without a doubt the most important edible species in Europe where it is sold in virtually every local market. Commercially it is dried and used as a flavouring for soups, the flavour is said to be enhanced by the drying process. Cap 6-18cm. Stem 4-22cm. Common. **Edible and excellent.**

Boletus edulis

Leccinum variicolor

Leccinum aurantiacum

Leccinum variicolor

*An uncommon mushroom which appears from late Summer through into Autumn growing very often on heathland in association with birch. Cap 5-15cm. Stem 5-15cm. Occasional. **Edible.***

Leccinum aurantiacum
Poplar Bolete

*The cap varies from tawny brown to orange, sometimes wrinkled and with an overhanging margin. The stem is white with small scales which become brownish with age. It grows in the soil of woodlands and heaths especially with aspens from summer onwards. Cap 5-18cm. Stem 8-16cm. Rare. **Edible.***

Leccinum versipelle
Orange Birch Bolete

*A large mushroom with a dull orange, dry and smooth cap. Once again the cap margin overhangs the pores. The stem is white and covered with small black-brown scales and, if opened up, the flesh will bruise greenish-blue. As the name suggests another one found with birch. Cap 8-20cm. Stem 8-20cm. Common. **Edible.***

Leccinum versipelle

Suillus luteus

Suillus luteus
Slippery Jack

The slimy cap is a rusty olive brown which becomes shiny when dry. The pores are a lemon yellow (luteus means yellow) on a whitish stem which is granular above the obvious ring. It is widespread and common in Britain and Northern Europe, growing in association with conifer trees. Cap 5-10cm. Stem 5-10cm. Common. **Edible but sometimes causes unpleasant reactions.**

Leccinum scabrum
The Brown Birch Bolete

A common and widespread mushroom whose caps vary in colour from olive-brown to clay-brown or buff. The pores are usually a dirty grey on a white or grey stem covered in black scales. it is always found with birch with which it forms a mycorrhizal relationship. Cap 4-16cm. Stem 8-20cm. Common. **Edible.**

Leccinum scabrum

structure called a hypha this branches a multitude of times until a web of hyphae is formed. This is known as mycelium. But the story doesn't end here and there is still a complicated process to be undergone before fruit bodies can be produced.

A precarious life then, and one which in addition to all the other pressures being brought to bear on the countryside, is subject, literally, to human greed.

Britain is a small island whose countryside is under threat from a variety of interests. More and better roads, houses, railways, airports and leisure facilities are the demands of an ever increasing and 'sophisticated' population. Fungi in common with everything else in the countryside, are vulnerable to these demands. They are also very susceptible to

Boletus subtomentosus

Suillus grevillei

Xerocomus chrysenteron
The Red-Cracked Bolete

It has an olive-brown velvety cap which cracks to reveal the pinky-red flesh underneath. The stem changes from yellow at the top to red at the base and the lemon yellow pores turn green when cut or bruised. It is found in deciduous woodlands from early summer to late autumn.
Cap 4-12cm. Stem 4-8cm. Common.
Edible.

Xerocomus chrysenteron

Boletus subtomentosus

Fairly common and widespread, found in mixed and deciduous (particularly birch) woods, from late summer to autumn. The cap is usually pale yellowish to olive brown with bright lemon yellow pores.
Cap 5-10cm. Stem 5-10cm.
Common. ***Edible.***

Suillus grevillei
The Larch Bolete

The cap surface is a striking yellow to golden brown and covered with gluten. The stem is similar in colour and when young often has a membrane known as a cortina enclosing the pores. This eventually ruptures to leave an irregular white ring above which the stem is reticulated. Found in larch woodlands from late Summer to Autumn. Cap 3-10cm. Stem 5-8cm. Common. ***Edible.***

Strobilomyces floccopus

Strobilomyces floccopus
Old Man of the Woods

In Britain this is a very rare mushroom found at only one or two sites. It appears from early Autumn growing under beech in calcareous soil and really cannot be confused with any other species. The colour ranges from whitish-grey through to black as here and the cap is covered with distinctive fibrillose scales that sometimes overhang the edge.
Cap 5-15cm. Stem 8-15cm.
Extremely rare and should never be picked.

the effects of acid rain not only directly but also when they grow in association with specific trees. If the tree dies, so too do the associated toadstools. And surely no other group of plants attracts the avid attentions of the gourmands in the way that fungi do.

No one would argue that the picking of a few toadstools here and there by a few people does a great deal of harm, but in recent years the 'food for free' philosophy has gained great popularity and very many people, overcoming the traditional British fear of the toadstool, venture forth each autumn to join in what has become an annual ritual of spot, pick and eat the edible toadstool. In some instances whole areas are completely denuded of edible species by people, sometimes coachloads of them, who carry away baskets brimming with Boleti, Chanterelles, Macrolepiotas, or Parasols, and other delicacies.

To 'hoover' and totally denude an area of fungi is to deny others the pleasure of seeing these lovely plants growing in their natural habitats. It also destroys a valuable food source for animals such as squirrels, rabbits, badgers, foxes and deer at a time when they are building up reserves for the winter.

Lactarius rufus

Lactarius rufus
Rufus Milkcap

A very common mushroom in coniferous woodland from summer through into autumn. One of the characteristics of the reddish-brown ('rufus') cap is that the umbo is often distinctly pointed. The whitish gills release copious amounts of milk when cut which initially tastes hot on the tongue but the sensation gradually becomes one of burning. Quite clearly this is an identification feature that you always let your companion make!
Cap 2-8cm. Stem 4-8cm. Common.
Inedible.

Lactarius torminosus
Woolly Milkcap

The cap is initially convex later becoming flattened with a depressed centre. The margin is notably hairy giving rise to the common name. The overall colour is pink with darker zoning and the gills are a pinkish-cream giving off a white milk that is hot and peppery. It is found usually with birch trees in woodlands and heaths from late summer to autumn. Torminosus means to cause colic.
Cap 4-10cm. Stem 4-10cm. Common.
Inedible and poisonous.

Lactarius torminosus

Lactarius deliciosus

Lactarius deliciosus
Saffron Milkcap

In England this is an uncommon mushroom found in only a handful of coniferous woodlands during Autumn. The gills are the same colour as the cap but turn green when bruised. If you put the milk onto a white linen handkerchief it will slowly change from orange to green. This is a good edible species but a word of warning, it is prone to infestation by maggots!
Cap 5-12cm. Stem 3-7cm.
Uncommon. **Edible and good.**

Lactarius britannicus

An uncommon member of the milk cap family with a very rich orange-brown cap and cream coloured gills. The white 'milk' very slowly turns yellow on a linen handkerchief. In Britain it is found under beech during the autumn. Cap 3-8cm. Stem 4-8cm. Uncommon. **Edibility unknown.**

Lactarius britannicus

Lactarius pyrogalus

Lactarius pyrogalus

The cap is at first convex becoming flattened and finally funnel shaped. It is an infrequent mushroom found on the soil in mixed woodland often under hazel. The milk is white and burns the tongue hence the name pyrogalus. Cap 5-10cm. Stem 4-6cm. Occasional. **Inedible.**

Lactarius serifluous

An uncommon member of the milk caps certainly in Britain where it is found in deciduous woodland under beech and oak. Cap 5-7cm. Stem 2-5cm. Uncommon. **Inedible.**

Lactarius serifluous

Coprinus atramentarius

Coprinus atramentarius
Common Ink Cap

It has a smooth conical cap with rusty coloured scales near the centre which give a brownish appearance. The gills are white but soon turn black producing an inky fluid as they deliquesce. Most of the Coprinaceae deliquesce, that is, on maturing the caps turn into an inky fluid which gives rise to the common description of ink caps. It is found in parks, gardens and commonland growing on buried wood. It can be eaten but produces very unpleasant reactions if consumed with alcohol In fact it is similar to the drug antabuse which is used in the treatment of alcholics.
Cap 4-10cm. Stem 4-12cm.
Common.
Edible with reservations.

Coprinus macrocephalus

Coprinus macrocephalus

I came across this rare coprinus one spring growing on a rotting straw bale. There were several specimens which had already started deliquescing, fortunately this one was still in pristine condition and worthy of being photographed.
Cap 1-3cm. Stem 3-7cm.
*Rare. **Inedible.***

Coprinus comatus
Lawyers Wig or
Shaggy Ink Cap

The tall cylindrical or bell shaped cap is white with a brownish centre and very obvious shaggy scales. Initially the gills are white slowly changing to pink and finally black as they delequesce from the bottom upwards and drip an inky fluid. These toadstools are very common. It is a good edible species but only while the gills are still white.
Cap 6-15cm. Stem 10-30cm.
*Common. **Edible and good.***

Coprinus comatus

Coprinus micaceus

Coprinus micaceus
Glistening Ink Cap

This is a widespread and common member of the ink caps which is found all year on dead and buried wood of broadleaved trees. Fawn-buff in colour the cap is at first covered with powdery granules which glisten (hence the common name) but these are washed off by rain.
Cap 2-5cm. Stem 4-10cm.
Very common. **Edible.**

Coprinus plicatilis
Little Jap Umbrella

This tiny enchanting toadstool is as fragile and delicate as it appears. The thin grooved cap is conical at first but then expands flat as the fungus matures. It can be found from spring onwards growing in grass on lawns. Cap 0.5-1.5cm. Stem 3-6cm. Common.
Edible but worthless.

Coprinus picaceus
Magpie Ink Cap

This is a very striking toadstool with its tall conical grey/black cap covered with patches of white veil remnants. It can grow to heights of 30cm on a slender white stem. It normally appears in autumn in deciduous woodland especially where beech is growing on chalk.
Cap 5-8cm. Stem 6-30cm.
Occasional. **Edible but worthless.**

Amongst professional mycologists opinion is split as to whether constant picking of fungi leads to their eventual decline. Many feel that the case is already proven and in countries such as France and Switzerland restrictions are put on how often and how much people can collect.

The gathering of toadstools on such a scale in Britain is a comparatively recent phenomenon and there has probably not been enough time yet to monitor and evaluate the full effects. It could well be that as long as the mycelium remains intact and can find the necessary nutrients, it will continue to produce fruit bodies. But equally there is the possibility that constant picking will eventually cause a colony to die out. And what effect does the trampling of many eager feet have on the surounding habitat?

Pleurotus ostreatus

Pleurotus ostreatus
Oyster Fungus

This is a widespread and common fungus which parasitises living deciduous trees mainly beech, often in large clusters as here. As you can see it is very photogenic. It can often be found throughout the year although it is more abundant in the autumn. It can vary quite considerably in colour and is a good edible species often found in supermarkets albeit supplied by commercial growers. P. cornucopiae has a preference for the stumps of oak and elm and is not as common as P. ostreatus.
Edible.

The study of fungi is still in its infancy. Many species have only recently been discovered to be beneficial to man (Penicillin is the most obvious example). The poisons in some species can be isolated and, in controlled doses, can be used to our advantage (for example, Ergot).

If toadstools contain chemicals similar to those used in rocket fuel and to control alcoholism then what other extraordinary properties are awaiting discovery? And how sad if these were never to be known to us.

The British Mycological Society is currently studying the problem of conservation and hopefully will come up with some guide lines in the near future.

In Britain, Authorities such as the Forestry Commission and the National Trust have for some time had bye-laws forbidding the collection of any plants on their properties. Surely the time has now come for the maxim 'moderation in all things' to be put into practice. Not many of the people gathering all this free produce actually need to do so. Nowadays it is possible to buy many different species of toadstools from the more specialist delicatessens and

Lentinellus cochleatus

supermarkets and the fungi that they sell are grown for the purpose. Certainly the thrill of the chase would be missing from this course of action but if we want to conserve our countryside and the plants and animals that depend upon it then at some time, and soon, we are going to have to exercise some self restraint - unpalatable though that may be!

The Birch Bracket and other useful fungi

Growing exclusively on birch, this bracket must surely be one of the easiest to identify. Milk chocolate in colour on the upper surface, the lower surface, when young, looking amazingly like a white marshmallow. The bracket is quite soft and squidgy when young with a curious putty-like texture. As the fruit body matures so it hardens and becomes firm and then, in extreme age, dry, brittle and worm eaten.

Pleurotus cornucopiae
Oyster Fungus

Very similar to P. ostreatus it is more funnel shaped and tends to grow in an upright fashion. This is a good edible species is cultivated and can be found in supermarkets under the heading of wild mushrooms. It is mainly found growing on fallen beech from early summer through to the first frosts. **Edible.**

Note: There are two species with the name Oyster Fungus

Pleurotus cornucopiae

Lepista nuda

Lepista nuda
Wood Blewitt

The gill colour ranges from lilac to violet. It grows almost anywhere in gardens, pastures and under hedgerows from late summer onwards.
Cap 5-12cm. Stem 5-10cm.
Common. **Edible and good.**

Tricholoma gambosum

Tricholoma gambosum
St. George's Mushroom

A spring mushroom that in Britain is traditionally gathered on the 23rd of April, St. George's Day.
It appears in the grass of lawns, meadows and pastures.
Cap 5-15cm. Stem 2-4cm.
Occasional. **Edible and good.**

Chroogomphus rutilus
Pine Spike Cap

A fairly common species with striking dark decurrent (running down the stem) gills and a bright yellow base to the stem. It grows on the soil in coniferous woodland especially under pines. Cap 3-10cm. Stem 5-10cm. Common. **Edible.**

Chroogomphus rutilus

Gymnopilus penetrans

Volvariella bombycina

Gymnopilus penetrans
Freckle-Gilled Gymnopilus

A very common toadstool found in conifer woodland growing on dead stumps and buried wood.
With maturity the golden brown gills become spotted or 'freckled' which gives rise to its English name. Cap 3-6cm. Stem 3-6cm. Common.
Inedible.

Volvariella bombycina
Silky or Tree Volvaria

This is both a parasitic and saprophytic fungus that grows on the roots and trunks (often in hollows) of deciduous trees. The cap is bell shaped, creamy white and covered with long straw coloured fibres which give it a shaggy appearance. The gills are white initially but later turn pink. Cap 5-20cm. Stem 5-15cm. Rare.
Edible.

Oudemansiella mucida

Fungi are not generally thought of as being useful apart from when concocting exotic culinary masterpieces. However, there are a few which provide exceptions to prove this particular rule. The birch bracket is one of these exceptions. Another English name for the plant is The Razor Strop fungus and indeed in days gone by this is exactly what it was used for. A square or slice of bracket would be nailed or glued to a board and a preparation of Fullers Earth applied to it. This provided a very efficient and successful 'sharpening stone' for the old cut-throat razors.

But the uses for this amazingly versatile fungus didn't end here. The Victorians who loved collecting things, found that if they cut it into small pieces it provided an effective medium on which to mount butterflies and other insects. It was also reputed to be very effective when used as corn plasters! But possibly the most delightful use to which it was put was as fuel for handwarmers. In the days when muffs were all the rage an efficient handwarmer could be made by cutting up pieces of Birch bracket, putting them in a tin and setting light to them before putting the lid on the tin. Birch bracket

Oudemansiella mucida
**Porcelain Fungus or
Poached Egg Fungus**

Initially the cap is bell shaped later becoming flattened and glutinous (slimy). Grey at first then white and translucent, sometimes with a yellowish centre. The stem is white and lined above the sticky ring. It grows on beech throughout the year and cannot be confused with any other species. It can be eaten provided the slimy mucus is first removed by washing. Cap 3-10cm. Stem 5-8cm. Common. **Edible.**

Oudemansiella mucida

Macrolepiota rhacodes

Macrolepiota rhacodes
Shaggy Parasol

*A pale buff-greyish cap that expands to almost flat and is covered with the shaggy scales that give rise to its common name. Very similar in many respects to M. procera but lacking the snake-like markings on the stem. Note the diagnostic snake-like markings on M. procera below. It grows in conjunction with conifers rather than in grassy places. Cap 6-20cm. Stem 10-20cm. Common. **Edible but can cause gastric upsets.***

smoulders rather than burns furiously and so would heat the tin and provide a sort of mini hot water bottle which must have been very cosy.

Rivalling the Birch bracket for usefulness is a material which comes from another bracket fungus, one which again is mainly found in association with Birch. This is the curiously shaped Fomes fomentarius, the Hoof fungus or Tinder fungus.

Pieces of the young fruit bodies were sliced, soaked and softened by being hit with a rolling pin or other suitable object. The resulting leathery matter has been used for such diverse things as making hats, wound dressings and perhaps most famously, for kindling fires. This miracle substance is known as Amadou, a name which is reputed to come from a French word meaning 'Something that sets one on fire'.

Macrolepiota procera

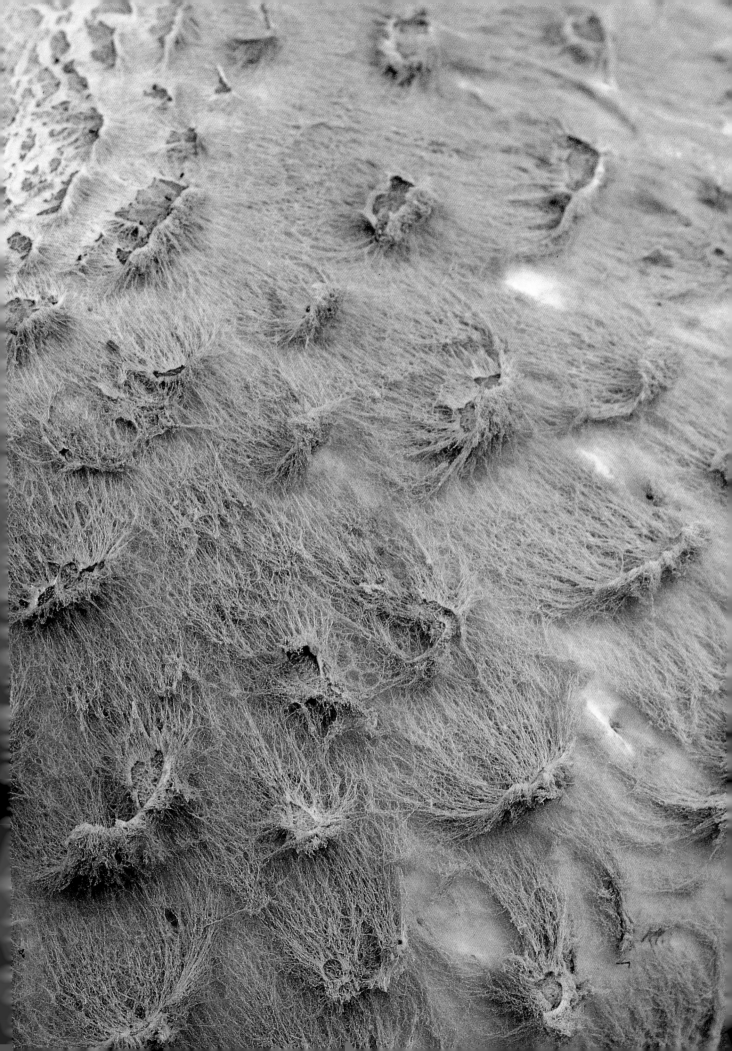

Lepiota cristata
Stinking Parasol

A very small and delicate mushroom with a creamy pink cap that has a chestnut central patch and reddish brown scales. The stem is white with an ephemeral ring but its most characteristic feature is it's strong and unpleasant smell! It grows from late summer in the grass in gardens, along roadsides and on heaths and commons.
Cap 1-5cm. Stem 2-8cm. Common.
Inedible and probably poisonous.

Lepiota cristata

Lepiota ventriospora

A small toadstool very similar in appearance to others within this group. The cap is covered with chestnut brown scales on a pale yellowish-brown ground supported by a scaly stem with an ephemeral ring. It grows on soil in woodlands especially where birch and beech predominate.
Cap 3-9cm. Stem 2-5cm.
Uncommon. **Edible but worthless.**

Lepiota ventriospora

Psathyrella hydrophila

This is a very common and widespread mushroom that grows, densely tufted, on the soil close to stumps or buried wood. The cap colour is variable and changes with the humidity.
Edible but unpleasant.

Psathyrella hydrophila

Paxillus atrotomentosus

Paxillus atrotomentosus
Velvet Footed Paxillus

The velvety cap is a rusty or reddish-brown, with an in-rolled margin. The gills are buff, deepening to a yellowish-brown with age and supported by a stout velvety stem. It grows during autumn on the stumps and dead wood of coniferous trees.
Cap 10-25cm. Stem 4-10cm.
Uncommon. **Inedible.**

Paxillus involutus
Roll Rim

The Roll Rim is a very common fungus appearing in a whole variety of habitats usually where birch is growing. When young the cap is tightly inrolled hence the common name. It has been widely eaten in the past but now the evidence suggests that it is one to leave alone.
Cap 5-15cm. Stem 5-10cm.
Common. **Poisonous.**

Paxillus involutus

Paxillus panuoides

Paxillus panuoides
Pale Paxillus

The caps are yellowy-brown and shell shaped under which are apricot yellow gills. The fruit bodies can be found during the autumn on the dead wood of conifers.
Cap 1-6cm. Common.
Inedible.

Harraps French dictionary contributes a nice little colloquialism 'Il prend feu comme de l'amadou' - He is very touchy' So amadou obviously flared up very easily and effectively!

Daldinia concentrica, Cramp Balls or King Alfred's cakes is yet another arsonist's delight. With a texture like charcoal and the ability to heat up very easily and quickly, this fungus is extremely useful for getting fires started. In the Middle Ages people used to believe that carrying one or two of the fruit bodies in a pocket would ward off cramp.

One of the effects that the rhizomorphs of Honey Fungus *(Armillaria mellea)* have on decayed wood could loosely be described as 'useful' though perhaps 'curious' is more apt. It is these bootlace strands and also the mycelium of the same fungus that are behind most of the sightings of luminous wood in Britain. Before the exact cause of this phenomenon was known, many explanations were attempted. Perhaps the most charming of these being that glow worms had crawled over the wood and left the light behind them. Gradually however people came to realise that a fungus was the culprit and it was noticed that the light continued only as long as the wood was

Laccaria amethystea

Laccaria laccata

Laccaria amethystea
Amethyst Deceiver

This pretty toadstool gets its name because of the way it's appearance changes depending on the weather and its age. The cap colour can be anything from a jewel-like amethyst to shades of dried up clay-brown. It grows from late summer in coniferous or deciduous woodland most often under beech.
Cap 2-6cm. Stem 5-10cm. Common.
Edible.

Laccaria laccata
The Deceiver

A small and very common toadstool whose variable colour and size 'deceives' time after time. The cap varies from dark pinkish tan to buff and even paler. The gills are pinkish fawn and widely spaced. It is common in woodlands, on heaths and in grass.
Cap 1-6cm. Stem 5-10cm. Common.
Edible.

Laccaria amethystea

Mycena polygramma

Mycena polygramma

A grey brown, grooved cap which is conical at first but flattening later still retaining an obvious umbo. The stem is conspicuously ridged and hairy at the base. It grows singly or in small groups usually in the debris of coniferous trees from late summer.
Cap 2-5cm. Stem 5-10cm.
Uncommon. **Inedible.**

wet. It is now realised that under these conditions the fungus would be able to continue to grow and it is only while it is living and growing that it produces the luminous effect. Once the wood dried out, growth would stop and the light would die.

There were many reports of luminous wood during the two world wars. Soldiers in the trenches used to put pieces on their helmets to avoid bumping in to each other in the dark. Some infected branches found on a country road were sent for official scrutiny at the highest level because it was feared they had been tampered with and were part of a fiendish plot to signal to the enemy. Some stacked wood in a London timber yard actually had to be covered over because it shone so fiercely it could have induced unwelcome attention from enemy planes.

Mycena galericulata
Bonnet Mycena

The cap is initially bell shaped but flattens out. Grey to greyish brown and lined at the margin. The stem is the same colour as the cap and noticeably hairy at the base. It grows all the year round in tufts on stumps and logs of deciduous trees especially oak.
Cap 2-8cm.
Stem 5-12cm. Common. **Inedible.**

Mycena galericulata

Mycena inclinata

Mycena haematopus
Bleeding Mycena

A pinky-brown cap that flattens out as the toadstool matures. The gills are whitish with a darker margin and the stem which is pinky-grey contains a blood red juice which oozes when the flesh is damaged. It grows in tufts on the wood of broadleaved trees during the autumn. Cap 1-4cm. Stem 5-10cm. Common. **Inedible.**

Mycena crocata
The Stainer

In Britain this tiny slender toadstool is uncommon and confined to beech woods growing on chalk. Whereas M. haematopus has blood-red latex or milk crocata has orange-yellow milk or latex which readily stains the fingers. It is found in the leaf litter often attached to fallen twigs. Cap 1-3cm. Stem 4-8cm. Uncommon. **Inedible.**

Mycena inclinata
Granny's Bonnets

One of my favourite fungi pictures mainly because of its simplicity. This group was growing in deep shade but I opted not to use flash, instead relying on a very long exposure of 30 seconds. It is found on the wood of broadleaved trees, especially oak, from late summer onwards. Cap 1-4cm. Stem 5-10cm. Common. **Inedible.**

Mycena haematopus

In other countries different species of fungus have been recorded as causing the same phenomenon. These are mainly members of the genus Pleurotus and, in America, Panus stipticus. This last is interesting as what is to all intents and purposes the same fungus grows in Britain but does not have the same luminous qualities. In the tropics luminous fungi are more common. Some are said to produce enough light to read by and were also used on occasions to mark paths through the forests.

Most people will have heard of truffles even if they have not actually sampled this much prized delicacy. Truffles are one of the few fungi which live entirely underground and this secret, subterranean existence gave rise to much theorising and speculation - How did a plant grow without roots?

Earth Stars

The Geastraceae are collectively and commonly referred to as earth stars and are closely related to the puffballs, certainly the method of spore dispersal is much the same. In Britain they are widespread and rare with less than ten species present. They grow in the soil (occasionally sand dunes) often in troops and appear from late summer onwards. Shown here are Geastrum sessile, Geastrum striatum and Geastrum triplex.
Not edible.

Geastrum striatum

Geastrum sessile

Clavulina rugosa
Wrinkled Club

Growing in small groups from summer to autumn on the soil in mixed woodlands. Fruit body 5-10cm. Common. **Edible.**

Clavulina rugosa

Clavulina cristata

Clavulina cristata
White Coral Fungus

The fruit body is white throughout and heavily branched. It grows in tufts on the soil in both broadleaved and coniferous woodlands from summer to late autumn. Fruit body 2-10cm. Common. **Edible.**

Clavulina cinerea
Grey Coral Fungus

The fruit body is pale grey to grey brown and is multi-branched. It grows on the soil in woodlands forming tufts or clumps which can be found from late summer through into autumn. Fruit body 2-10cm. Common. **Edible.**

Clavulina cinerea

Ramaria stricta

***Ramaria stricta*
Straight-Branched Coral
Fungus**

*In common with the ramarias or
'coral' fungus it produces the spores
on the surface of the multi-branched
fruit body. The flesh is yellow but
slowly turns to wine red if bruised.
It grows from late summer on dead
wood and stumps of both coniferous
and broadleaved trees. Fruit body
4-10cm. Common.* **Inedible.**

Was it a plant at all when it had no branches, flowers, fruits, etc. How did it come to be in the ground in the first place? Were these strange excrescences formed by thunder and rain, by lightning, by liquid from trees or were they simply the children of the gods?

While there may have been disagreement on this point, it seems there was none on the esteem in which these apparently magical plants were held. An esteem which was and still is based on the fact that these are amongst the most highly prized culinary delicacies in the world.

For hundreds of years truffles have been much sought after and a certain romance has sprung up around them. What could be more evocative than stories of laden camel trains arriving in Damascus; of stalls in bustling markets in North Africa; of Greece and Rome, of Cedar forests and Spanish meadows.

But although truffles were known and prized in other countries, it was not until the seventeenth century in Rushton Northamptonshire that the first British record occurred and even then, as many of the trees in the park in question were

Calocera viscosa

Calocera cornea

Calocera cornea

*Very common found on the dead
rotting wood of broadleaved trees
from summer to autumn. This
group was growing on a felled beech
trunk. Note that the rubbery yellow
fruit bodies are un-branched unlike
the closely related C. viscosa.
Fruit body 0.5-1.5cm. Common.*
Inedible.

Calocera viscosa
Yellow Antler Fungus

*This is a very beautiful and
photogenic fungus as I hope this
picture conveys. Common and
widespread, it grows throughout
the year peaking during autumn.
It is specific to logs and stumps in
coniferous woodland.
Fruit body 3-7cm. Common.*
Edible but indigestible.

introduced from France it was not entirely certain that these truffles were native.

That such a highly prized delicacy was so well hidden undoubtedly produced many problems and so it was that truffles came to provide a rather unusual source of employment. Throughout the eighteenth and nineteenth centuries, indeed until as recently as 1935, truffle hunting was a recognised profession.

Truffles give off a strong scent which attracts animals to them and therefore it quickly became apparent that the surest way to track down the much desired prey was to utilise this fact. Several animals including goats and bear cubs are said to have been press-ganged into action but the most well known are pigs who rootle around in the leaf litter and are then withdrawn, enticed away by alternative food, once the prize has been found.

However, trained dogs were held by many to be more efficient. Usually of the poodle variety, though any other easily trained and manageable make would do, dogs had the reputation of being more energetic and obedient and were reputedly able to concentrate for longer.

In 1789 Gilbert White recorded that the price being asked for

Baeospora myosura

a truffle was half a crown. Obviously inflation then wasn't what it is today for in Victorian times the price appears to have been anything from the same 2/6d (25p) to four shillings (40p) a pound.

In addition to the use of sniffer dogs, two other methods of detection were known to country people. One was to look for gnats which, attracted by the smell, would dance in groups just above the surface of the earth covering the truffles. The other method, perhaps marginally less esoteric, was to observe the ground in a likely spot and look for the distinctive radiating cracks and small mounds of soil which were reliable indicators.

There must have been a great deal of excitement and enjoyment in the search for, detection of and capture of the prize and it is therefore dismaying to read in 1995 of the invention of an electronic device which will now do the job with mechanical and clinical efficiency and speed. How typical of this impatient and greedy age that all chance and indeed all romance should be swept aside. But then the pace of present day life does not allow for a gentle rummage

Baeospora myosura
Pine Cone Fungus

This is one of the group of small toadstools which grow on buried or partially buried conifer cones. This one grows specifically on pine cones from autumn to winter and is fairly widespread.
Cap 0.5-3.5cm. Stem 1.5-5cm. Uncommon. **Inedible.**

Paneolus semiovatus
Dung Mottle-Gill

No doubt about the host material for this toadstool. I found this specimen half-way up a mountain on which sheep were grazing in Southern Ireland. It has a white silky stem with a ring and a bulbous base should you care to investigate! It is a widespread and common fungus growing from spring onwards always on dung.
Cap 1-5cm. Stem 5-15cm. Common. **Inedible.**

Tricholoma sulphureum

Tricholoma sulphureum
Gasworks Tricholoma

The cap stem and gills of this attractive toadstool are all sulphur yellow, the cap flattening with age. The most striking feature however is its strong, tarry smell of coal gas which is unmistakable.
It is widespread and common being found in woodlands from late summer.
Cap 2-8cm. Stem 5-10cm. Common.
Inedible possibly poisonous.

Crucibulum laeve
Common Bird's Nest Fungus

The fruit body of this remarkable fungus looks just like a miniature bird's nest with eggs. Initially the 'eggs', called peridoles and containing the spores, are covered by a pale yellow membrane. This eventually ruptures and disappears thus allowing the spores to be released. It can be found virtually anywhere growing on dead twigs and other debris from late summer to autumn.
Fruit body 0.5-1cm across Peridoles 0.1-0.2cm Common.
Inedible.

through the leaves on a blue and gold autumn day or for time to lie squinting into the sun trying to find a tell-tale band of ecstatically gyrating flies. Could it be that today's price of £300 or more per kilo has something to do with the more prosaic approach?

That many fungi are useful, in some cases life-saving (Penicillin was discovered by Alexander Fleming in 1928 and its practical uses developed some 10 years later) is not in doubt. What is not clear is how many species, some still unknown, we will destroy before we have had a chance to find out what properties they possess. Only recently it has been discovered that minute filamentous fungi, so small they can only be seen under a powerful microscope, actually make substances called zaragozic acids which could possibly be

Hypholoma fasciculare

used to prevent coronary heart disease by inhibiting the accumulation of the fatty deposits which lessen the flow of blood through the coronary arteries.

Not long after the Chernobyl disaster it was discovered that some species of fungi appear to have the ability to concentrate radioactive particles. High on the list is the Bay Bolete (*Xerocomus badius*) one of the most widely gathered and eaten toadstools. What was even more interesting was that the isotope levels found in these species was not consistent with the idea that Chernobyl was responsible for this tainting and therefore the radioactivity must have been around before the accident.

Some fungi spend their entire lives in termite nests, others are dependent on certain species of ants for their survival - what other fascinating facts will come to light if only we give ourselves the time to find out?

Hypholoma fasciculare
Sulphur Tuft

One of the most common toadstools in Britain. It grows throughout the year in large clumps on the dead wood of broadleaved and coniferous trees. The sulphur yellow caps flatten with age. Cap 2-7cm. Stem 4-10cm. Common. **Inedible.**

Clitocybe geotropa
Trumpet Clitocybe

This is a common fungus especially on calcareous soils under broadleaved trees where it grows either solitary or in groups quite often forming rings. These are young specimens shown at the umbonate stage (umbo literally means having a bump in the cap), later the cap will become depressed and can grow up to 20cm in diameter. Cap 4-20cm. Stem 5-15cm. Common. **Edible and good.**

Clitocybe geotropa

Kuehneromyces mutabilis

Kuehneromyces mutabilis
Two-Toned Pholiota

The caps are an attractive brownish-orange, umbonate and dry out from the centre to a much paler buff colour. The stem darkens towards the base and has a scaly ring.
It grows in tufts on dead wood and, as I hope this picture shows, can be very photogenic.
Cap 3-6cm. Stem 3-8cm. Common.
Edible.

Kuehneromyces mutabilis

Pholiota carbonaria
Charcoal Pholiota

Clearly this fungus is aptly named. Here it is growing on the remnants of a burnt out beech stump. Normally the cap colour is brown to tan but in the picture the colour has been leeched out by heavy rain. It is found during autumn but can occasionally be found throughout the year, often growing on bonfire sites. Cap 2-5cm. Stem 3-8cm. Common. **Inedible.**

Pholiota carbonaria

Pholiota alnicola

Pholiota alnicola

The lemon yellow cap is at first convex then flattens out. It is invariably sticky with a yellow stem which is darker towards the base. It grows on wood such as birch, willow and alder either singly or in groups. P. aurivella is similar and also inedible. Cap 2-6cm. Stem 3-8cm. Uncommon. **Inedible.**

Pholiota aurivella

Bolbitius vitellinus
Yellow Cow Pat Toadstool

This is a delicate and fragile toadstool which initially is a bright chrome yellow gradually fading to pale fawn with age. As its name suggests it can often be found on dung but I have also found it on wood shavings. In this photograph it is growing on an old straw bale. It can be seen anytime from spring onwards growing either singly or in small groups.
Cap 0.5-5cm. Stem 2-5cm.
Common.
Edible but worthless.

Bolbitius vitellinus

Lacymaria velutina
Weeping Widow

The English name was given to this toadstool because of the black 'tears' which it weeps as it matures. The gills which are initially brown, become black with age. It grows in the soil on path edges, amongst grass and woodland from late spring through to autumn. Cap 2-10cm. Stem 4-10cm. Common.
Edible but very bitter.

Pholiota squarrosa
Shaggy Pholiota

A straw coloured mushroom with both the cap and stem covered by upturned shaggy scales. The yellow flesh has a faint smell of radish when bruised and is edible provided it is cooked thoroughly. It is common and found during autumn growing on both living and dead wood.
Cap 6-12cm.
Stem 5-8cm. Common.
Edible.

Lacymaria velutina

Pholiota squarrosa

Tricholomopsis rutilans

Tricholomopsis rutilans
Plums and Custard

The plum part of this delightfully pretty toadstool's name refers to the vinaceous red or plum coloured scales which cover the cap surface which is actually yellow. However, it is the saffron yellow gills which provide the custard. The stem is yellow like the cap and similarly covered with scales although they are less dense. It grows exclusively on the wood of conifers from late summer on.
Cap 3-12cm. Stem 3-10cm. Common. **Inedible.**

Tricholoma fulvum
Yellow-Brown Tricholoma

Fairly common and widespread found in deciduous woods particularly with birch during the autumn. The sticky chestnut brown cap flattens with age but still retains a low umbo. The stem is the same colour as the cap with straw coloured gills that are sometimes spotted brown with age.
Cap 3-12cm. Stem 3-7cm. Common.
Edible but only just.

Tricholoma fulvum

Tricholoma terreum

Tricholoma terreum
Grey Tricholoma

A fairly common species in coniferous woodland growing in the litter from late summer through to autumn. There is some dispute about the edibility of this species so it is worth remembering the general rule that says that all grey Tricholomas should be avoided.
Cap 2-8cm. Stem 4-8cm. Common.
Inedible.

Gymnopilus junonius
Orange Pholiota

This is a common and widespread beautiful golden orange toadstool with caps that are covered in small fibrillose scales. The gills which are golden at first become rusty-brown. It tends to grow in tufts on dead wood from late summer through into autumn.
Cap 6-15cm. Stem 5-15cm.
Common. **Inedible.**

Hebeloma crustuliniforme
Poison Pie

This is a very common and widespread mushroom appearing from late summer through into autumn. It much prefers to grow in open and mixed woodland.
It grows on a whitish stem and the flesh smells strongly of radish.
Cap 4-10cm. Stem 6-15cm.
Common. **Poisonous.**

Gymnopilus junonius

Hebeloma crustuliniforme

Omphalina postii
You have to look hard to find this tiny toadstool which often grows in moss or on bonfire sites. The gills are yellowish and widely spaced and it can be found from spring onwards.
Cap 2-6cm. Stem 2-8cm. Rare.
Inedible.

119

Hygrocybe Subglobispora

Hygrocybe coccinea

Hygrocybe coccinea
Scarlet Hood

The bell shaped cap is a vivid blood red and the stem is the same. Widespread and found in the grass of parks, playing fields and garden lawns from summer to autumn. Cap 1-5cm. Stem 2-5cm. Common. **Inedible.**

Hygrocybe subglobispora

Like Hygrocybes coccinea it grows in grass from late spring through into autumn. Cap 2-6cm. Stem 3-8cm. Rare. **Inedible.**

Hygrocybe nigrescens
Blackening Wax Cap

The orange cap is often irregularly shaped and will gradually turn black with age along with the stem. It appears during the autumn growing in grass. Cap 2-5cm. Stem 3-8cm. Occasional. **Inedible.**

Hygrocybe nigrescens

121

Podoscypha multizonata

Auricularia auricula
Jew's Ear Fungus

A very common and widespread fungus growing on deciduous trees and shrubs, particularly elder. Although I see this fungus every year this is the only example that I have found that really lived up to its common name. It is a good edible mushroom and sold in huge quantities by chinese delicatessens. In fact, the first time I ever knowingly ate this fungus was in a Chinese restaurant in Turkey. Fruit body 2-10cm Common.
Edible.

Auricularia auricula

Podoscypha multizonata

This attractive and rare fungus looks very like one of the ornamental cabbages that are becoming increasingly popular with many gardeners today. It grows rosette-like from a single tough leathery stem forming upright fan-shaped 'ears'. It is initially buff to chestnut brown turning dark red with age. It grows on the ground in deciduous woodlands during the autumn, standing through into the winter months. Fruit body 5-20cm. Rare.
Inedible.

Stereum hirsutum

Stereum hirsutum
Yellow or Hairy Stereum

A very beautiful fungus that is both widespread and common throughout the year. It is very variable colour-wise depending on the age of the fruit body and the season. It grows on the dead wood of broadleaved trees in irregular tiered brackets which have a covering of hair.
Fruit body 2-10cm. Common.
Inedible.

Coriolus versicolor
Turkey Wings or Many Zoned Polypore

Common throughout much of the world this is a variable bracket fungus which forms clusters of overlapping tiers on dead wood. The colour can vary greatly but normally it comprises zones of grey, brown and green always with a white margin. It can be seen all year. Caps 3-10cm. Very common.
Inedible.

How to Photograph Fungi

The fundamental principle behind my fungi photography is to produce images that are true to nature, pictorial whenever possible, reveal the diversities of both form and colour and, last but not least, are as technically near-perfect as they can be.

Invariably, I prefer to photograph fungi in their natural environment rather than bring lifeless specimens back to the studio. And, unsurprisingly, I prefer to use daylight as the basis for my exposures. In my opinion, there is no substitute for natural light and the delicate nuances it can impart to a photographic image. Of course, there are occasions when I am forced to use flash, but only rarely do I rely on it entirely to obtain a picture. Much of the time, I am balancing light from the flash with the ambient light in such a way that, hopefully, you – the viewer – do not realize it has been used.

In the following sections, I offer guidelines on the materials, equipment and basic techniques you require to successfully photograph fungi.

Equipment and materials

The first camera I ever purchased was a Canon 35mm SLR, and I have remained loyal to Canon ever since. My initial choice was made purely by chance. Today, as a professional wildlife and nature photographer of 16 years' standing, I have the technical expertise to make the necessary comparisons between every camera system currently on the market. At this point in time, I consider there to be no finer system for the serious nature photographer than Canon; if there is, I can assure you I would be using it.

I own a complete and comprehensive range of lenses – 13 at the last count – from a 20mm ultra wideangle to the mighty 600mm f4L super-telephoto that, alone, weighs a staggering

6½kg. Clearly, I would not get very far if I tried to carry them all with me every time I went on a field trip, although I often come across nature photographers who, loaded down like pack horses, seem intent on doing just that.

I am a firm believer that comfort plays an important part in all aspects of nature photography and certainly the less I have to carry, the better. My younger colleagues attribute this to age but I argue for the value of experience. To this end, I have devised various equipment combinations – field kits, if you like – to specifically cover the subjects I intend to photograph on a particular trip. (See my current field kit, right, for photographing fungi.)

The camera body

Today, the range of 35mm SLR cameras on the market is huge and, as each new model comes on the market, it boasts a greater degree of sophistication over its predecessor. Many of these hi-tech features are irrelevant to mushroom photography, with autofocus perhaps being the most obvious example. It would probably be top of the list for bird photography but, apart from aiding a photographer with failing eyesight, it plays little or no part in the pursuit of fungi.

I have therefore listed, in no specific order, those features that I consider most useful. My preference at this time is for the Canon EOS1N body and I normally carry two of them with me; the main reason for this being that, if one breaks down, I have a spare as a back-up. I also utilize both bodies simultaneously, with Fuji Sensia loaded in one and Fuji Velvia in the other. Very often, I take the identical shot on both cameras and select the best image later.

Through-the-lens (TTL) metering

This is an extremely important feature that really comes into its own when the quality of the light is constantly altering. When this happens, the metering system in the camera monitors the light and automatically adjusts the exposure accordingly. It will also convert the exposure whenever you add an extension tube or converter.

Aperture priority mode

I consider this mode (along with manual priority mode, below) to be essential for fungi photography. In fact, I work in aperture priority mode for most of my general nature photography, and probably 80% of the time when photographing fungi.

FUNGI FIELD KIT

2 x EOS1N bodies
20–35mm zoom
50mm macro
100mm macro
180mm macro
Extension tubes
300EZ flashgun
Off-camera lead
Uni-Loc tripod
Arca B1 ball & socket head
Exposure meter
Film
Assorted reflectors
and diffusers
Lee filter system
Spare batteries
Remote release
Beanbag
Plastic sheet
Kodak Gray Cards
Angle finder
Tamrac backpack

Manual priority mode

This mode allows you to take complete control of the exposure and set both the aperture and shutter speed individually. This is vital, especially when you have a subject that falls outside of medium tone, ie. white or black. In addition, when using flash it is essential to be able to manually set a speed that does not exceed the flash sync speed.

Metering modes

Most cameras offer a choice of metering modes. The main three are as follows:

- overall multi-segment pattern, commonly referred to as 'evaluative' by Canon and 'matrix' by Nikon that measures the entire scene.

- centre-weighted average metering also measures the entire scene, but places a greater emphasis on the central portion of the frame.

- spot metering takes a reading of only 1–2% of a scene.

Of the three, I use only evaluative and spot metering. I find the latter most useful as it allows me to take a reading from the mushroom cap alone, should that be necessary.

Exposure compensation

In the case of non medium-toned subjects, the ability to dial-in autoexposure compensation is useful but not essential, as it can easily be done by manually setting the compensated exposure.

Autowind

This is a must! Coupled with a cable or electronic release, autowind allows you to take several consecutive frames without having to handle the camera; thus reducing the likelihood of accidentally ruining the focus or the composition.

Depth of field preview

Another essential feature that allows you to stop the lens down to the selected aperture prior to taking the picture, and thus check that the depth of field is sufficient for the subject. It also has an additional benefit: as you stop down, the viewfinder image darkens and any highlights are revealed – dried grass, stems or leaves, for example. These can be removed, or 'gardened', so as to avoid any detrimental effects on the final result.

Mirror lock

Only available on a very few camera bodies, this feature

My standard fungi photography set up: the camera plus 100mm macro lens supported on the Uni-Loc tripod and Arca B1 ball and socket head. Also shown is the Lee filter holder with its indispensable angle finder and bellows-style lens hood.

allows you to lock up the reflex mirror prior to taking the shot. A single lens reflex camera generates a degree of internal vibration whenever the shutter is fired and this can adversely affect the sharpness of a photograph, especially at slow shutter speeds. These internal vibrations are caused by two separate mechanical actions, first as the mirror swings upwards then as the shutter opens and closes.

If you want to experiment with the level of shock and vibration in your camera, run this simple test. Using an empty camera body, set a shutter speed of 1/30th of a second. Put the camera to your mouth so that your top front teeth are in contact with the camera's hot shoe, and fire the camera. You will immediately feel any problems.

Major problems arise when working at slow shutter speeds with macro or telephoto lenses. These lenses not only magnify the subject but also any faults, too – in this case, the shock and vibrations – which result in pictures that are not sharp. By using the mirror lock-up facility, the vibration is substantially reduced.

Self-timer

The self-timer option, while not essential, can be very useful, especially when you do not have a remote release facility, as it allows for a short time delay before the camera fires a shot. This inhibits any vibration caused by handling the camera, and is best deployed when the camera is mounted on a tripod.

There are normally two time-delay options: 2 seconds or 10 seconds. In my opinion, the latter is the best for fungi photography. On some cameras, the timer mechanism also locks up the mirror before the time-delay begins – something that is not always apparent – so make sure you check your camera's manual. You may already have a mirror lock-up facility without being aware of it.

Focusing screens

I insist upon this option on a camera. Plain, bright matte screens are undoubtedly the best choice as they do not interfere with composition and they make focusing much easier. I prefer those that incorporate a fine grid overlay; the reference lines help you to level up the horizon and also enable you to double-check that your verticals remain vertical in the final picture.

Viewfinder

Do beware that what you see in the viewfinder is 100% of what appears on the film. Many cheaper cameras show as little as 92% of the image which means that your final picture may well include distracting material around the edges of the frame. You can of course crop out extraneous material at printing stage, but if you give talks and show slides as I do, continually cropping and remounting every other transparency is a real pain.

Some viewfinders incorporate another useful feature. Some of the latest cameras have a dioptre adjustment facility especially for people who use glasses for reading. If your eyesight is not 100%, it results in sharper pictures.

Viewfinder shutter

Again, choose a camera that incorporates this useful facility. The shutter prevents stray light entering through the back of the camera when your eye is not looking through the viewfinder. On sunny days, any light entering in this way can adversely affect the exposure and result in ruined slides.

Lenses

100mm macro

Of my four regular lenses, I use the 100mm macro for the majority of my close-up studies of fungi, and there is no doubt that if I was restricted to using one lens only, it would be this one. I guarantee that any nature photographer worth his or her salt will have this lens (or its equivalent), in their camera bag. If you are just starting out in nature photography, this macro lens is the one to buy.

50mm macro

The 50mm macro becomes necessary when, for example, you want to shoot directly above a cluster of fungi and your tripod is already set at its maximum height, thereby discounting the 100mm macro with its narrower field of view. I also use the 50mm macro as a longer wideangle especially as it stops down to f/32, giving you the option to maximize the depth of field in scenic shots.

180mm macro

The very narrow field of view of the 180mm macro allows you to isolate your subject even further, and is very effective if you want to eliminate extraneous vegetation from an image, or take out invasive patches of skyline. Because it allows you to work at a greater distance from your subject, it means you can also avoid your own shadow impinging on the image, or trampling on other plants.

20–35mm zoom

The 20–35mm wideangle zoom is at its best when you encounter large clusters such as the gregarious Sulphur Tuft, or when you want to compose a smaller image of the main subject in its habitat. Very often, you can achieve a more pictorial and informative result by combining the two. Compare the Sulphur Polypore shots (or, commonly, Chicken of the Woods) taken in an ancient Yew forest at Kingley Vale in Sussex (page 47). When I first came upon this superb specimen, I took the close-up shot using the 180mm macro – at one point I even climbed the tree to get shots from every angle. It was only when I had finished and was preparing to move on that I saw what turned out to be 'the definitive image'. This photograph epitomizes the kind of image I continually strive for, but only rarely achieve.

Extension tubes

I carry two extension tubes with me: 25mm and 12mm. When mounted to one of the macro lenses, either singularly or coupled together, these allow me to get in really close for a detailed study – of the cap or gills, for instance.

Angle finder

An angle finder is one of those wonderful gadgets that, once used, forces you to wonder how you ever managed without it. How many times do you mount the camera at ground level – virtually 90% of the time with fungi – only to find that, in order to see through the viewfinder, you have to prostrate yourself on the ground, often in muddy conditions – or worse? (See opposite.) One answer is to carry a plastic sheet. I also use mine to rest my backpack on in wet conditions. However, the best solution is to purchase an angle finder so that you can compose your picture in comfort.

When buying an angle finder, a useful tip is to make sure the one you select gives exactly the same size of image as that seen through the camera viewfinder. Be warned: some of the cheaper versions present the image upside down and back to front. Needless to say, this makes composition very frustrating, if not impossible.

Film

Beauty, as we all know, is in the eye of the beholder and, in some ways, the same applies to one's choice of film. As subjects, fungi lend themselves quite nicely to black and white reproduction, but I much prefer working in colour. Generally, much of the appeal of nature photography is taking true-to-life images in natural colour. We all see colours differently so, initially, my advice is to use whatever brand of film pleases you most, whether that be slide or negative film.

I work exclusively in slides because, as a professional photographer, the pictures I take are intended for commercial use in books, magazines and elsewhere, and I have to meet the demands of publishers for top quality reproduction. Printers much prefer to work with colour transparency, quite simply because slow slide film produces sharper images, has greater colour saturation and less visible grain in comparison with other types of film. Slides are the accepted currency these days; very few picture libraries and agencies take prints.

Lying down on the ground to photograph mushrooms in the middle of a wood or field is a sure way of attracting attention.

For many years, my favoured slide film was Kodachrome and many of the pictures in this book were shot on K25 or K64. However, in the last five years or so, I have uniformly switched my allegiance to Fuji and, at present, almost exclusively use Sensia 100 and Velvia.

Velvia has highly saturated colours which, for landscape photography, are very attractive. But beware, with some natural history subjects – birds in particular – they can appear too 'over the top' or artificial. I would never consider using it in bright sunny conditions, but, perhaps obviously, it works well when the light is overcast and dull. It can produce startling images that really jump off the light box.

I like Sensia for many reasons: it performs well in bright light, it is low in contrast, and is extremely fine grained, all of which produces very sharp, natural-looking results. It is also especially good when pushed. In fact, although Sensia is available in several speeds, I only buy the ISO 100 and, when lighting dictates, push the film one or two stops rather than buy ISO 200 or ISO 400. I find this a far better proposition; the faster films show far too much grain for my liking.

A useful tip when pushing the film one stop is to rate the film at 200, as you might expect. However, when pushing 2 stops, rate it at 320 rather than 400 and continue to instruct the lab to push it 2 stops, otherwise your slides will return slightly underexposed. Pushing the film, however, is mainly reserved for using long lenses that demand fast shutter speeds and is only rarely required for photographing fungi.

Flash

I carry the lightweight Canon 300EZ flashgun with an off-camera TTL lead as standard. I always use the flash off-camera because, by doing so, I can position it where it will have the best effect. Invariably, I will use it in conjunction with one or more reflectors, or fire it through a diffuser.

When using flash, I am usually striving for a pleasing balance with the ambient light (available natural daylight). This can mean having to reduce the flash output by anything up to 2½ stops over the ambient exposure. An important factor to take into account when using the flash as a fill-in light, is to check the gun's manual to see whether the manufacturer already has a daylight exposure compensation built-in as a default setting. If it has, remove it; otherwise, when you dial-in ⁻1 stop, you will almost certainly fail to achieve your desired effect. Modern flashguns today – the Canon Speedlights 430, 540,

Gymnopilus penetrans
Freckled-gilled Gymnopilus

It is rare for me to use flash as the total basis for the exposure but in this instance I had no other option. This cluster of Freckled-gilled Gymnopilus, Gymnopilus penetrans, was growing in total darkness. Coupled with a low viewpoint, flash saved the day and gave me a super result.

Having taken the first image without a flash I decided to experiment, especially as these Mycenae are translucent and lend themselves to backlighting. For the second shot, I set the daylight exposure manually on the camera and then reduced it by one stop. This has the effect of darkening the background and some of the foreground, except where the flash hits. Using the off-camera lead, I then fired the flash behind the group, angled in from the left-hand side. This is a nice result, with the exception of the highlighted slug trail which detracts from the image. Sometimes, experimentation gives you more than you bargained for.

550 and the Nikon SB 24, 25, 26, for example – have dial-in exposure compensation facilities.

Don't despair if your particular brand does not have this facility; provided that it has TTL (through-the-lens flash metering), you can easily fool your flashgun into producing a reduction in power. To do this, you must first take the ambient exposure and set that manually on your camera, making sure that you select a shutter speed that will synchronize with your flash. If you next double your film speed setting in the camera, you are effectively telling the flash that the film is one stop faster than it really is, and the flash responds by reducing its output by one stop accordingly. Re-doubling the film speed – for example, from ISO 100 to 400 – will reduce its output by 2 stops, and so on.

I also use fill-in flash to improve the colour temperature of the light in shady conditions, to knock out shadows in sunny conditions, or to subtly reduce the exposure on the background. I rarely use flash as the sole light source of the exposure. Generally, I want the flash to be invisible on the final image.

Teleflash

This is a relatively new item to many nature photographers, although the idea has been around for some time. I first bought one made by the German manufacturer, Metz, several years ago. It fits over my large 60CT4 hammer guns that I use in conjunction with long telephoto lenses when photographing nocturnal creatures such as owls or foxes.

A teleflash unit works as follows. If you place a Fresnel screen about 6–8in in front of the existing one on your flashgun, it narrows and concentrates the beam of light. It has the effect

Phellinus igniarus
False Tinder Fungus

This was taken on one of those dreadful days when using the flash is essential, resulting in a striking picture of the False Tinder Fungus, Phellinus igniarius. The difficult conditions are evident in the initial record shot; there is little light from a dull grey sky directly behind the subject. By exposing the subject correctly, the sky, background trees and vegetation are all overexposed producing a result that warrants a quick despatch to the bin.

of increasing the power of the gun by 2–3 stops as well as projecting the flash beam over a much greater distance. For photographing fungi, its use is restricted to brackets growing high up in the trees.

Today, lightweight and extremely cheap teleflash versions are available to fit most of the flashguns currently on the market and are essential for the nature photographer. The one I use is manufactured in the US, weighs about 3oz and actually folds up and fits in my breast pocket.

Filters

I have used the Lee filter system for many years now and, in my opinion, there is no finer system on the market. The main

Polyporus squamosus
Dryads Saddle

The classic bracket fungus Dryads Saddle, Polyporus squamosus, growing beneath a green woodland canopy. (For green woodland canopy, read green filter.) Adding an 81b warming filter for the second shot restores the natural light and colour to which our eyes adjust – but the film does not.

filters I use for photographing fungi are: a polarizer, an 81 series of warming filters and a set of graduated neutral density filters. All three types can be used individually or in combination to make subtle alterations to the final image, without being glaringly obvious.

Polarizer

In strong sunlight, the polarizer effectively lowers the contrast by reducing glare and improving colour saturation. When it rains or the subject is wet, it will cut through reflections, once again boosting colour. A downside to using this filter is that it can reduce the light reaching the film by as much as 2 stops.

Warming filters

The warming filters (81a, b and c), do just as their names suggest and warm up colour in the image, which is often essential on those dull grey days or beneath a green woodland canopy. Remember, when light is passing through green leaves they act in the same way as a green filter. Under these conditions, the human eye automatically adjusts and we are unable to see any difference, but film does not adjust and records the light with a colour cast.

Neutral density filters

I use the graduated neutral density filters to tone down the extreme contrasts between bright skies or backgrounds and the subject. This is a common problem, especially when you are shooting with a wideangle lens to include a portion of sky or background and the subject is growing in deep shade.

Batteries

Take plenty of batteries! There is nothing worse than taking pictures in the middle of nowhere (often the case with fungi photography), the camera's battery runs out and you discover that you have not brought a spare. The same applies to the flashgun. I always carry far more batteries on a shoot than I am ever likely to need. Very occasionally, I resort to using a Quantum turbo power pack.

Remote release

A remote (or cable) release is simply an electronic (or mechanical) device that allows you to fire the camera without handling the camera body. It is twice as effective when combined with mirror lock-up or a self-timer.

Where slow exposures are concerned, it is almost impossible not to impart some vibration when manually pressing the shutter button. This is contentious in relation to long lenses. When I am photographing birds with a long telephoto lens, contrary to most books on the subject, I never use one. However, I use one all the time for fungi photography, in conjunction with a tripod. With a beanbag support, I prefer to stabilize the camera by using my finger to fire the shutter while pressing down firmly on the camera body.

Supports

Uni-Loc tripod

One of the secrets to producing consistently pin-sharp work using slow films is to have a good-quality tripod. All the pictures in this book were taken with the camera supported either on a tripod or a beanbag; in fact, the majority of them would have been impossible to take without one or the other.

Over the years, I have reached the conclusion that there is no single tripod or tripod head that is perfect for every aspect of nature photography and, as a consequence, I have several. However, some years ago I was asked to field-test a British tripod prior to its launch and, to this day, I have used no other for photographing fungi. It is the Uni-Loc tripod (very similar to the Benbo) which might have been designed specifically for fungi photography, it's that good.

Arca head

In conjunction with my Uni-Loc tripod, I use an Arca Swiss B1 ball-and-socket head incorporating a quick-release plate: without doubt the finest ball-and-socket head currently on the market. It is infinitely preferable to using a pan-and-tilt head: who wants to tighten three screws when you can just tighten one?

Beanbags

Perhaps a surprise to many people, beanbags are often far better than a tripod when working on fungi at ground level. If you can, use one filled with polystyrene beads instead of the conventional beans or rice; it works just as well and is much lighter to carry. As I have already mentioned, it is also a good idea to carry a small piece of polythene to place under your beanbag in wet conditions.

Very often in damp, boggy woodland, the ground can be very soft and springy and consequently not provide very stable foundations for your tripod. In these conditions, try to push the legs down into the ground and then suspend your loaded camera bag from the apex. Both these measures will go some way to providing extra stability – and so improve your chances of getting a razor-sharp picture.

As you can see, this group of Common Puffballs, *Lycoperdum perlatum*, are growing at ground level and the photographer has chosen this angle to photograph them. In this situation, any tripod will be unstable because the legs need to be spread to such a degree that the head will flex, thereby reducing your chances of obtaining a sharp image. This is where a beanbag scores over the tripod every time. Notice that the photographer is hand-holding the camera and not using a cable release.

Kodak Gray Card

Correct exposure is the essence of good photography, especially critical for slide film where you have less latitude for error. The Kodak Gray Card (produced in America hence the trade name spelling), reflects 18% of ambient light falling on it. This enables you to achieve the perfect middle tone upon which all camera and light meters are based and an invaluable aid in the tricky lighting situations so often encountered in fungi photography. I would not be without one.

Reflectors and diffusers

Reflectors can radically improve your fungi pictures. I use the Lastolite 12in and 20in ones, which are silver on one side and gold on the other. They are lightweight and collapsible for ease of packing and carrying. I supplement these with a range of smaller sizes that I make myself. The beauty of using a reflector to add fill-in light as opposed to flash is that you can see the effects instantly and, if necessary, change them.

Apart from adding extra light, the larger reflectors can be used to reduce the overall contrast in the scene. They also make excellent windbreaks. Smaller ones placed judiciously can be used to reveal important details of the gills or the stipe (stem) that might otherwise be shaded out by the cap. Simple reflectors of different sizes can be made from crumpled aluminium cooking foil, which is then re-flattened and mounted onto cardboard. You can also use the reverse side of the Kodak Gray Card, thereby multiplying its usefulness.

Lastolite also make collapsible diffusers and these are really useful in strong sunlight. Positioned between the sun and the subject, they eliminate heavy shadow and reduce contrast. They are extremely effective when flash is fired directly through them, providing soft, even, shadowless light.

Exposure meter

I carry a hand meter and favour the Sekonic L-308B. While I generally use the Kodak Gray Card and rely on the camera's internal meter, there are times when a second, alternative exposure reading is useful, to confirm what the camera is telling you – thereby giving you peace of mind.

Ganoderma applanatum
Artist's Fungus

A silver Lastolite 20in reflector is required to illuminate the underside of this common bracket called the Artist's Fungus, Ganoderma applanatum. In the second shot, the reflector reveals the spore mass – an important element that is not visible in the first shot. Note that the original exposure has not been changed as we can clearly see from the background, it is simply the reflector that makes the difference.

Optional kit

Occasionally, it is wise to carry some optional extras in your camera kit to avoid disappointment.

I sometimes come upon a bracket fungus growing so high in the tree that it requires a long telephoto lens to obtain an acceptable image size. When this occurs, and provided the subject warrants it, I simply return in the following day or two with an appropriate lens. This is possible because brackets tend to remain in good photographic condition for longer – or rather, have a better shelf-life than other fungi (if you excuse the pun). However, when the venue is a long way from home and I think there is a good chance of finding examples of bracket fungi, I take my 400mm f5.6 lens, together with a 1.4 converter. I also take along the more powerful 550EZ Canon Speedlight flashgun and couple this with a lightweight teleflash attachment.

OPTIONAL EXTRAS

400mm telephoto lens
1.4 converter
Teleflash
550EZ Cannon Flash

Battarraea phalloides
Sandy Stilt Puffball

You must bracket a shot if you want to guarantee a perfect exposure every time. These slides show the results of bracketing by ⅔ of a stop, which is my preferred method. The subject is the very rare Sandy Stilt Puffball, Battarraea phalloides. Having driven 120 miles to see this fungus, I was not coming back without a perfectly exposed series of shots.

Techniques

Exposure

Getting a perfectly exposed slide each and every time you press the shutter button is, without doubt, the most difficult task facing any amateur or professional photographer. By 'perfect exposure' I mean a slide that returns from the processors exactly as you wanted it to look when you took the picture. The resultant image may look under or overexposed to someone else, but that is simply their opinion. If the image has come out the way you wanted it to, then it is a perfect exposure.

If you accept this premise then it surely follows that you alone, not your camera, should decide on the exposures. The meter reading is a good starting point but there will be many times when you override the exposure suggested by the meter. Once you acknowledge this, you are on your way to becoming a better photographer. To help you learn to judge for yourself, try 'bracketing' the exposure suggested by the meter reading, a technique routinely used by professional photographers to ensure they capture the perfect image.

There are many kinds of fungi that grow in open grassland or common land where getting the correct exposure is relatively easy. Unfortunately, the vast majority grow in woodland, often in minimal light and sometimes in deep shade. Arriving at the correct exposure under these conditions can be a daunting task for even the most competent photographer. Perhaps the most difficult and classic example is a white mushroom set against a very dark background. Spot metering will give you the answer, but not as you might think. If you take the spot reading off the white cap and use that exposure, the resultant slide will be underexposed. By the same token, take it from the background and the subject will be overexposed. To overcome this problem, the solution is quite straightforward. First compose and focus your picture and then, without altering the focus (very important), place a small Kodak Gray Card in front of your mushroom, take a reading from that and set it manually on the camera. Consider this is your base exposure from which you can now reduce to allow for the pale colour of the subject: I would suggest ½–⅔ of a stop in dull conditions and 1–1⅓ stops on a bright day.

If, however, the reading requires an exposure lasting longer than one second, then you are still in trouble and you will need to refer to the following paragraph before you press the shutter.

Reciprocity failure

This is the deadly trap that lies in wait for the fungi photographer. Under normal circumstances, an exposure reading of 250th of a second at f/8 can easily be altered to an equivalent exposure, such as 125th of a second at f/11 or 500th of a second at f/5.6 or even as far as 2000th of a second at f/2.8. All these settings would result in a correctly exposed picture. This convenient arrangement is called reciprocal and it allows us to select an aperture or shutter speed to suit the subject.

Problems arise when the exposure time is one second or longer because this can cause the reciprocal arrangement between the shutter speed and f/stop to break down, hence the term 'reciprocity failure'. Without going into a full technical explanation, it simply means that the rate at which the film absorbs light slows down and, as a consequence, you have to allow more time than indicated by the camera meter. Most manufacturers supply the reciprocity compensation required for their own film types which varies between manufacturers and their individual brands. In addition, some advise using filters with very long exposures to correct colour shifts and it is essential that you consult the manufacturer of your own brand of film for their specific recommendations. Fortunately, with the films I currently use, I have found filtration unnecessary but I do make adjustments to the exposures (see panel, below right).

These are the results of my experience and produce the results that suit me. However, I recommend that you do your own tests regardless of whether or not you use the same film brand.

In order to remember these allowances, I have printed them out onto a credit card-sized piece of cardboard and laminated it. Actually, it is a dual-purpose memory 'jogger' because on the reverse I have the numerous EOS1N camera custom functions that I use because they are impossible to remember. I have produced several of these cards and carry them in various places so that I can always find one when I need it.

COMPENSATION VELVIA

1 second: None
4 seconds: + ⅓ stop
8 seconds: + ½ stop
16 seconds: + ⅔ stop
32 seconds: + 1 stop

SENSIA 100

16 seconds: None
32 seconds: + ½ stop

The two shots of the tiny Mycenae shown here were both taken with a 100mm macro at f/22. The first shot was taken at 1/1 (or life-size) and quite clearly the depth of field (0.09in) is insufficient to cover all the caps and stems. My solution was to move backwards and accept a smaller image. In the second shot, you can see that I now have all three subjects in focus.

Depth of field

Many photographers have a problem understanding the principles of depth of field (DOF) and the important role it plays on the final image. Quite simply, the depth of field in a photograph is an invisible band of focus that lies parallel to the film plane. Any subject or subjects falling inside this band appear in focus, anything outside it appears out of focus. Clearly, the first priority, especially with macro lenses, is to ensure that the principle subject being photographed (in our case fungi), is as parallel to the film plane as possible.

Provided you do not change your camera position or change lenses – in other words, maintaining a constant image size – a small aperture such as f/16 will give a wider band of focus than a larger aperture of, for example, f/4. The main problem with macro lenses is that they are often used to magnify the image size and, when they do, the depth of field is substantially reduced, to mere fractions of an inch. For example, if we use a 100 macro lens at f/22 to photograph the subject at half life-size, the depth of field is only 0.26in. If you consider a mushroom with a cap size of 1in in diameter, you can see that we will have only marginally more than a quarter of it in focus.

By pushing in our depth of field preview button, we can actually see how much of our subject lies within the band of focus and whether it is sufficient. When it is not, there are two ways to increase it. The first is to stop the lens down even further, to f/22 or f/32. If this fails, the second option is to reduce the image size either by moving further away from the subject or to swap lenses for one with a shorter focal length.

The presentation of our subject in relation to its habitat can be controlled by choice of aperture. By selecting f/22 for the first shot of this Boletus, the background is slightly out of focus but still identifiable, particularly the pile of logs. Notice the change when we open the aperture to f/5.6. The background is now completely out of focus and diffuse, making the subject stand out almost three-dimensionally. This is known as 'differential focusing'.

Gardening

This is the nature photographer's term for 'tidying up' the area within the frame as seen through the viewfinder prior to taking the shot. All too often, the mushroom is surrounded or partially obscured by living and dead vegetation. The dilemma is whether to remove any of it and at what point do you stop?

I have no qualms about selective gardening, provided that it does not require the removal of other growing fungi or plants, and if the end results strengthen and focus attention on the subject. It is very frustrating to have your slides returned only to find them marred by an out of focus stem of dry grass that might easily have been removed at the time.

Once all extraneous matter has been 'gardened', a good tip is to have one final look through the viewfinder with the lens stopped down. This will instantly reveal any of the less obvious highlights that you may have overlooked. On very bright days, however, stopping down the camera in this way instantly darkens the image and your eyes are unable to adjust. When this happens, the secret is to press and hold down the stop button at full aperture and then gradually wind down the lens to the selected f/stop. Often, potentially offending material is revealed long before you reach the chosen aperture.

Sometimes, the decision to garden or not can be quite difficult. There have been times when, having done so, I have instantly regretted it. Today, being older and wiser, in marginal situations such as these I simply take 'before' and 'after' shots and then enjoy the luxury of selecting the best shot on the light box.

When removing extraneous material from the frame of the viewfinder, try not to remove anything that is growing. In this instance, I hid the oak shoot on the left under the dead leaves. This is what I would describe as 'marginal 'gardening'. I take 'before' and 'after' shots and make my final decision as to which is best back home on the light box. Today, if necessary, I can scan it into the computer and 'garden' it even more using a program like Adobe Photoshop.

Composition

To try and define exactly what makes a good composition is impossible. People will often say to me 'It's all right for you, you have a good eye for a picture.' Well, perhaps I have, but I can assure you I was not born with this perceived ability. In fact, my 'eye' has had considerable training over the years, taking thousands of pictures. What I can say, is that there are no hard-and-fast rules to achieving good composition because there are simply too many variables to take into account. I can, however, give you some guidelines that will help.

All too often I see participants on my workshops who take one or two shots and are then champing at the bit looking for the next one (or perhaps the next fix?). So, my first piece of advice is to relax, and take your time. The fungi are not going anywhere!

Armillaria mellea
Honey Fungus

My advice is simple: when in doubt take both. With this particular clump of Honey Fungus, Armillaria mellea, I used at least two rolls of film. While taking the pictures, I varied both the composition and viewpoint, making absolutely sure that I took both vertical and horizontal images, left and opposite respectively, and this resulted in a tremendous selection of pictures.

Before setting up, remove the camera from the tripod and, holding it by hand, view the mushroom from every side and angle to decide which is the best. Remember the 'rule of thirds' and apply that. Many fungi fall into the toadstool category, ie. a round cap on top of a stem and, as such, lend themselves to a vertical composition. Take care when showing the whole plant that you do not crop any part of it with the edge of the frame. Bear in mind that the majority of fungi you come across will never end up as prize-winning pictures and learn to recognize those that will. What you leave out of the picture can often be as important as what you decide to leave in. In this context, the old saying 'less is more' is so often true. Sometimes, there is more than one potentially great picture. If in doubt, take more than one, varying the composition and viewpoint. You can always select the best later.

I judge an image quite simply. If, when I look at it, I say to myself 'I wish I had taken that', then that, for me, is a great picture. Looking at and studying other photographers' work is a good way to learn and improve your own. Hopefully, when you look at some of my pictures you, too, might say 'I wish I had taken that'.

Flammulina velutipes
Velvet Shank

When you have mushrooms growing in large clusters and in close proximity to one another as with this Velvet Shank, Flammulina velutipes, it pays to take a range of different shots using different lenses. In the first shot (top left), I have used the wideangle zoom lens to show exactly how and where they were growing, plus the habitat. In the next (top right), I have moved in close and used the 50mm macro to show the different clusters together. Finally, with the 100mm macro (left), I have concentrated on a single cluster.

Ionotus dryadeus
The Weeping Polypore

Some great images can be found by moving in real close on fungi as I have done here with Ionotus dryadeus. This eye-catching shot, as well as being visually intriguing, exemplifies its common name The Weeping Polypore.

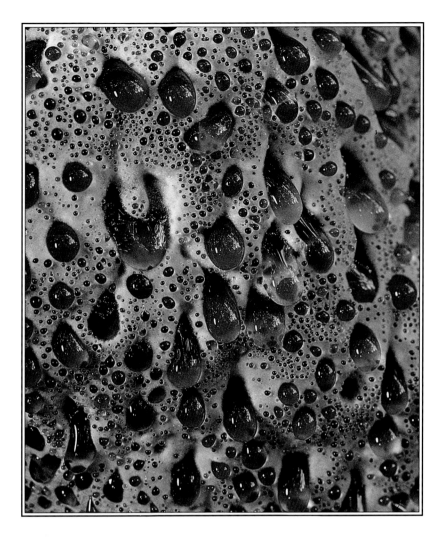

When labelling your fungi slides (and, indeed, when filing them), it is imperative that you work by the Latin name. This should always appear first at the top of your slide. The reason for this is quite simple. Of the three thousand or so fungi species common to Britain less than 5% actually have common names and these can vary from place to place. Take Coprinus comatus, for example, a member of the ink-cap family, which has at least two common names: the Lawyers Wig and the Shaggy Ink Cap. Another example is Coriolus versicolor, which is known as the Many Zoned Polypore in England, but in the US is called the Turkey Tail. It makes sense, therefore, to work in Latin and you will find, if you go on a foray, the leader will do exactly the same when naming specimens brought for identification.

COPRINUS COMATUS
The Shaggy Ink Cap
Ebernoe Common Sussex England UK
© GEORGE McCARTHY   105414

Where and when to find fungi

It comes as a surprise to many people that fungi are present throughout the year in Britain. Some are only found in the spring, such as St George's mushroom and the Morels. Nevertheless, the most rewarding time of the year is undoubtedly late summer and autumn before the frosts commence. Ideally, a good summer followed by a warm and wet autumn will produce the ideal growing conditions; fungi then appear everywhere, from garden lawns to parks, heaths and open meadows. The bulk are found in woods and forests with ancient deciduous mixed woodland such as the New Forest, which, in England, supports the most species. In fact, the vast majority of these fungi will actually be living in symbiosis with specific trees.

To find the best fungi locations in your area, contact your nearest Natural History Society or Wildlife Trust. In the autumn, look in your library for details of forays that might be taking place locally. Check out magazines and other publications for fungi workshops; I run several each year and there will be others. You might like to consider joining the British Mycological Society which organises forays all over the UK as a means to discover locations further afield.

Undoubtedly, one of the best ways to improve your fungi photography is to go a workshop led by someone who is not only a proficient photographer, but has a good knowledge of mycology. Details of these workshops, including my own, can be found in specialist magazines. Not only will you receive top professional advice, you will learn a lot about fungi and how to find them. The chances are you will also have an opportunity to visit some top fungi locations.

And finally…

There was a time when I only photographed fungi when I came across them by chance and then I would struggle, often in vain, to identify them. Today, I actively seek them out and look forward to the main autumn season and the rich harvest it brings. I still struggle to name them and I always experience a thrill when I photograph a new species.

In the last year, I have had the good fortune to photograph, among others, four superb rarities: Grifola umbellata in St Leonard's Forest, Sussex, Clathrus archeri in Kew Gardens, the associated Clathrus ruber at Bosham on the Sussex coast (see images, left, top to bottom) and, finally, Battarraea phalloides while standing on a pavement in the heart of Norwich – which just goes to show, you never know where you will find one next!

Fungi are a unique and fascinating group of plants, unlike any other on earth. Sadly, because they are so little understood, many of the rarer species are desperately in need of protection. In the UK, an upsurge in the trend for consuming wild mushrooms, exacerbated by an apparently insatiable glut of cooking programmes on television, has led to the proliferation of commercial collecting. In many areas such as the New Forest and parts of Scotland, the sheer volume of this type of collecting is surely having devastating results on the environment (see bottom left). Who can predict what the long-term effects will be? I can only advise that, if you wish to forage for mushrooms that you ensure their future survival by keeping your activity to a minimum, and if you have a photographic interest in fungi, that you take care to respect the fungi and their environment.

This book is illustrated with over 200 colour photographs of fungi, many of them full-page plates, which I hope inspire a much wider interest in, and study of, this fascinating branch of natural history.

About the author

One of the UK's leading professional nature photographers, George McCarthy is also an author, lecturer, tour leader and consultant specializing in British wildlife and the countryside. Since becoming a professional photographer in 1986, his photographs have appeared regularly in leading magazines and books, both in the UK and abroad. They also appear in calendars, posters, postcards and advertisements, and have been used by prestigious companies and organizations such as Kodak, Canon and the RSPB.

From his home in West Sussex, England, he runs his own tour company, Nature Photography Pro-Tours Ltd and, independently, travels far and wide in search of fresh subjects and images. The first six months of 2001, for example, saw him on tour photographing Snow Geese and Sandhill Cranes at the famous Bosque del Apache refuge in New Mexico. Following that, he led two consecutive tours to Florida's Everglades photographing alligators and, after a brief sojourn in the UK, travelled to Greece to photograph wildlife on the beautiful island of Lesvos.

Photographing fungi may seem rather tame by comparison, but for George it is a passion. He is a superb technician, happy to share his trade secrets in the hundred-plus lectures and workshops he gives each year to camera clubs and natural history societies. However, it is abundantly clear from some of the stunning images in this book that there is a quality in his work that transcends technique. He has a keen ability to capture and reveal the subject at its pictorial best. Like other top photographers around the world, he is able to see rather than just look, and this book is a fine example of his inspiring talent.

If you want to find out more about the work of George McCarthy visit him at **www.georgemccarthy.com**.

Directory of fungi

Index

TITLES AVAILABLE FROM
GMC Publications
BOOKS

WOODCARVING

The Art of the Woodcarver	*GMC Publications*
Beginning Woodcarving	*GMC Publications*
Carving Architectural Detail in Wood: The Classical Tradition	
	Frederick Wilbur
Carving Birds & Beasts	*GMC Publications*
Carving the Human Figure: Studies in Wood and Stone	*Dick Onians*
Carving Nature: Wildlife Studies in Wood	*Frank Fox-Wilson*
Carving Realistic Birds	*David Tippey*
Decorative Woodcarving	*Jeremy Williams*
Elements of Woodcarving	*Chris Pye*
Essential Woodcarving Techniques	*Dick Onians*
Lettercarving in Wood: A Practical Course	*Chris Pye*
Making & Using Working Drawings for Realistic Model Animals	
	Basil F. Fordham

Power Tools for Woodcarving	*David Tippey*
Relief Carving in Wood: A Practical Introduction	*Chris Pye*
Understanding Woodcarving	*GMC Publications*
Understanding Woodcarving in the Round	*GMC Publications*
Useful Techniques for Woodcarvers	*GMC Publications*
Wildfowl Carving – Volume 1	*Jim Pearce*
Wildfowl Carving – Volume 2	*Jim Pearce*
Woodcarving: A Complete Course	*Ron Butterfield*
Woodcarving: A Foundation Course	*Zoë Gertner*
Woodcarving for Beginners	*GMC Publications*
Woodcarving Tools & Equipment Test Reports	*GMC Publications*
Woodcarving Tools, Materials & Equipment	*Chris Pye*

WOODTURNING

Adventures in Woodturning	*David Springett*
Bert Marsh: Woodturner	*Bert Marsh*
Bowl Turning Techniques Masterclass	*Tony Boase*
Colouring Techniques for Woodturners	*Jan Sanders*
Contemporary Turned Wood: New Perspectives	
in a Rich Tradition	*Ray Leier, Jan Peters & Kevin Wallace*
The Craftsman Woodturner	*Peter Child*
Decorating Turned Wood: The Maker's Eye	*Liz & Michael O'Donnell*
Decorative Techniques for Woodturners	*Hilary Bowen*
Fun at the Lathe	*R.C. Bell*
Illustrated Woodturning Techniques	*John Hunnex*
Intermediate Woodturning Projects	*GMC Publications*
Keith Rowley's Woodturning Projects	*Keith Rowley*
Making Screw Threads in Wood	*Fred Holder*
Turned Boxes: 50 Designs	*Chris Stott*
Turning Green Wood	*Michael O'Donnell*

Turning Miniatures in Wood	*John Sainsbury*
Turning Pens and Pencils	*Kip Christensen & Rex Burningham*
Understanding Woodturning	*Ann & Bob Phillips*
Useful Techniques for Woodturners	*GMC Publications*
Useful Woodturning Projects	*GMC Publications*
Woodturning: Bowls, Platters, Hollow Forms, Vases,	
Vessels, Bottles, Flasks, Tankards, Plates	*GMC Publications*
Woodturning: A Foundation Course (New Edition)	*Keith Rowley*
Woodturning: A Fresh Approach	*Robert Chapman*
Woodturning: An Individual Approach	*Dave Regester*
Woodturning: A Source Book of Shapes	*John Hunnex*
Woodturning Jewellery	*Hilary Bowen*
Woodturning Masterclass	*Tony Boase*
Woodturning Techniques	*GMC Publications*
Woodturning Tools & Equipment Test Reports	*GMC Publications*
Woodturning Wizardry	*David Springett*

WOODWORKING

Advanced Scrollsaw Projects	*GMC Publications*
Beginning Picture Marquetry	*Lawrence Threadgold*
Bird Boxes and Feeders for the Garden	*Dave Mackenzie*
Complete Woodfinishing	*Ian Hosker*
David Charlesworth's Furniture-Making Techniques	
	David Charlesworth
David Charlesworth's Furniture-Making Techniques – Volume Two	
	David Charlesworth
The Encyclopedia of Joint Making	*Terrie Noll*
Furniture-Making Projects for the Wood Craftsman	
	GMC Publications
Furniture-Making Techniques for the Wood Craftsman	
	GMC Publications
Furniture Projects	*Rod Wales*
Furniture Restoration (Practical Crafts)	*Kevin Jan Bonner*
Furniture Restoration: A Professional at Work	*John Lloyd*
Furniture Restoration and Repair for Beginners	*Kevin Jan Bonner*
Furniture Restoration Workshop	*Kevin Jan Bonner*
Green Woodwork	*Mike Abbott*
The History of Furniture	*Michael Huntley*

Intarsia: 30 Patterns for the Scrollsaw	*John Everett*
Kevin Ley's Furniture Projects	*Kevin Ley*
Making & Modifying Woodworking Tools	*Jim Kingshott*
Making Chairs and Tables	*GMC Publications*
Making Chairs and Tables – Volume 2	*GMC Publications*
Making Classic English Furniture	*Paul Richardson*
Making Heirloom Boxes	*Peter Lloyd*
Making Little Boxes from Wood	*John Bennett*
Making Screw Threads in Wood	*Fred Holder*
Making Shaker Furniture	*Barry Jackson*
Making Woodwork Aids and Devices	*Robert Wearing*
Mastering the Router	*Ron Fox*
Minidrill: Fifteen Projects	*John Everett*
Pine Furniture Projects for the Home	*Dave Mackenzie*
Practical Scrollsaw Patterns	*John Everett*
Router Magic: Jigs, Fixtures and Tricks to	
Unleash your Router's Full Potential	*Bill Hylton*
Router Tips & Techniques	*GMC Publications*
Routing: A Workshop Handbook	*Anthony Bailey*
Routing for Beginners	*Anthony Bailey*

The Scrollsaw: Twenty Projects — *John Everett*
Sharpening: The Complete Guide — *Jim Kingshott*
Sharpening Pocket Reference Book — *Jim Kingshott*
Simple Scrollsaw Projects — *GMC Publications*
Space-Saving Furniture Projects — *Dave Mackenzie*
Stickmaking: A Complete Course — *Andrew Jones & Clive George*
Stickmaking Handbook — *Andrew Jones & Clive George*
Storage Projects for the Router — *GMC Publications*

Test Reports: *The Router* and *F & C* — *GMC Publications*
Veneering: A Complete Course — *Ian Hosker*
Veneering Handbook — *Ian Hosker*
Woodfinishing Handbook (Practical Crafts) — *Ian Hosker*
Woodworking with the Router: Professional
  Router Techniques any Woodworker can Use — *Bill Hylton & Fred Matlack*
The Workshop — *Jim Kingshott*

CRAFTS

American Patchwork Designs in Needlepoint — *Melanie Tacon*
A Beginners' Guide to Rubber Stamping — *Brenda Hunt*
Beginning Picture Marquetry — *Lawrence Threadgold*
Blackwork: A New Approach — *Brenda Day*
Celtic Cross Stitch Designs — *Carol Phillipson*
Celtic Knotwork Designs — *Sheila Sturrock*
Celtic Knotwork Handbook — *Sheila Sturrock*
Celtic Spirals and Other Designs — *Sheila Sturrock*
Collage from Seeds, Leaves and Flowers — *Joan Carver*
Complete Pyrography — *Stephen Poole*
Contemporary Smocking — *Dorothea Hall*
Creating Colour with Dylon — *Dylon International*
Creative Doughcraft — *Patricia Hughes*
Creative Embroidery Techniques Using Colour Through Gold — *Daphne J. Ashby & Jackie Woolsey*
The Creative Quilter: Techniques and Projects — *Pauline Brown*
Cross-Stitch Designs from China — *Carol Phillipson*
Decoration on Fabric: A Sourcebook of Ideas — *Pauline Brown*
Decorative Beaded Purses — *Enid Taylor*
Designing and Making Cards — *Glennis Gilruth*
Glass Engraving Pattern Book — *John Everett*
Glass Painting — *Emma Sedman*
Handcrafted Rugs — *Sandra Hardy*
How to Arrange Flowers: A Japanese Approach
  to English Design — *Taeko Marvelly*
How to Make First-Class Cards — *Debbie Brown*
An Introduction to Crewel Embroidery — *Mave Glenny*
Making and Using Working Drawings for Realistic
  Model Animals — *Basil F. Fordham*
Making Character Bears — *Valerie Tyler*

Making Decorative Screens — *Amanda Howes*
Making Fairies and Fantastical Creatures — *Julie Sharp*
Making Greetings Cards for Beginners — *Pat Sutherland*
Making Hand-Sewn Boxes: Techniques and Projects — *Jackie Woolsey*
Making Knitwear Fit — *Pat Ashforth & Steve Plummer*
Making Mini Cards, Gift Tags & Invitations — *Glennis Gilruth*
Making Soft-Bodied Dough Characters — *Patricia Hughes*
Natural Ideas for Christmas: Fantastic Decorations to Make — *Josie Cameron-Ashcroft & Carol Cox*
Needlepoint: A Foundation Course — *Sandra Hardy*
New Ideas for Crochet: Stylish Projects for the Home — *Darsha Capaldi*
Patchwork for Beginners — *Pauline Brown*
Pyrography Designs — *Norma Gregory*
Pyrography Handbook (Practical Crafts) — *Stephen Poole*
Rose Windows for Quilters — *Angela Besley*
Rubber Stamping with Other Crafts — *Lynne Garner*
Sponge Painting — *Ann Rooney*
Stained Glass: Techniques and Projects — *Mary Shanahan*
Step-by-Step Pyrography Projects for the Solid Point Machine — *Norma Gregory*
Tassel Making for Beginners — *Enid Taylor*
Tatting Collage — *Lindsay Rogers*
Temari: A Traditional Japanese Embroidery Technique — *Margaret Ludlow*
Theatre Models in Paper and Card — *Robert Burgess*
Trip Around the World: 25 Patchwork, Quilting
  and Appliqué Projects — *Gail Lawther*
Trompe l'Oeil: Techniques and Projects — *Jan Lee Johnson*
Wax Art — *Hazel Marsh*

GARDENING

Auriculas for Everyone: How to Grow and Show Perfect Plants — *Mary Robinson*
Beginners' Guide to Herb Gardening — *Yvonne Cuthbertson*
Bird Boxes and Feeders for the Garden — *Dave Mackenzie*
The Birdwatcher's Garden — *Hazel & Pamela Johnson*
Broad-Leaved Evergreens — *Stephen G. Haw*
Companions to Clematis: Growing Clematis with Other Plants — *Marigold Badcock*
Creating Contrast with Dark Plants — *Freya Martin*
Creating Small Habitats for Wildlife in your Garden — *Josie Briggs*
Exotics are Easy — *GMC Publications*
Gardening with Wild Plants — *Julian Slatcher*
Growing Cacti and Other Succulents in the
  Conservatory and Indoors — *Shirley-Anne Bell*

Growing Cacti and Other Succulents in the Garden — *Shirley-Anne Bell*
Hardy Perennials: A Beginner's Guide — *Eric Sawford*
Hedges: Creating Screens and Edges — *Averil Bedrich*
The Living Tropical Greenhouse: Creating a Haven for Butterflies — *John & Maureen Tampion*
Orchids are Easy: A Beginner's Guide to their
  Care and Cultivation — *Tom Gilland*
Plant Alert: A Garden Guide for Parents — *Catherine Collins*
Planting Plans for Your Garden — *Jenny Shukman*
Plants that Span the Seasons — *Roger Wilson*
Sink and Container Gardening Using Dwarf Hardy Plants — *Chris & Valerie Wheeler*
The Successful Conservatory and Growing Exotic Plants — *Joan Phelan*

PHOTOGRAPHY

An Essential Guide to Bird Photography — *Steve Young*
Field Guide to Landscape Photography — *Peter Watson*
Light in the Landscape: A Photographer's Year — *Peter Watson*
Outdoor Photography Portfolio — *GMC Publications*

Photography for the Naturalist — *Mark Lucock*
Viewpoints from *Outdoor Photography* — *GMC Publications*
Where and How to Photograph Wildlife — *Peter Evans*

VIDEOS

Drop-in and Pinstuffed Seats	*David James*	Twists and Advanced Turning	*Dennis White*
Stuffover Upholstery	*David James*	Sharpening the Professional Way	*Jim Kingshott*
Elliptical Turning	*David Springett*	Sharpening Turning & Carving Tools	*Jim Kingshott*
Woodturning Wizardry	*David Springett*	Bowl Turning	*John Jordan*
Turning Between Centres: The Basics	*Dennis White*	Hollow Turning	*John Jordan*
Turning Bowls	*Dennis White*	Woodturning: A Foundation Course	*Keith Rowley*
Boxes, Goblets and Screw Threads	*Dennis White*	Carving a Figure: The Female Form	*Ray Gonzalez*
Novelties and Projects	*Dennis White*	The Router: A Beginner's Guide	*Alan Goodsell*
Classic Profiles	*Dennis White*	The Scroll Saw: A Beginner's Guide	*John Burke*

MAGAZINES

WOODTURNING ✦ WOODCARVING ✦ FURNITURE & CABINETMAKING
THE ROUTER ✦ WOODWORKING
THE DOLLS' HOUSE MAGAZINE ✦ WATER GARDENING
OUTDOOR PHOTOGRAPHY ✦ BLACK & WHITE PHOTOGRAPHY
BUSINESSMATTERS

The above represents a full list of all titles currently published or scheduled to be published.
All are available direct from the Publishers or through bookshops, newsagents and specialist retailers.
To place an order, or to obtain a complete catalogue, contact:

GMC Publications,
Castle Place, 166 High Street, Lewes, East Sussex BN7 1XU, United Kingdom
Tel: 01273 488005 Fax: 01273 478606
E-mail: pubs@thegmcgroup.com

Orders by credit card are accepted